THE FIRST FATHER

Abraham:
The Psychology
and Culture of a
Spiritual Revolutionary

Henry Hanoch Abramovitch
Department of Behavioral Science
Sackler School of Medicine
Tel Aviv University, Israel

UNIVERSITY
PRESS OF
AMERICA

Lanham • New York • London

Copyright © 1994 by
University Press of America®, Inc.
4720 Boston Way
Lanham, Maryland 20706

3 Henrietta Street
London WC2E 8LU England

Library of Congress Cataloging-in-Publication Data

Abramovitch, Henry Hanoch.
The first father : Abraham : the psychology and culture of a spiritual
revolutionary / Henry Hanoch Abramovitch.
p.   cm.
Includes bibliographical references and indexes.
1. Abraham (Biblical patriarch)—Psychology.   2. Isaac (Biblical
patriarch)—Sacrifice.   3. Bible. O.T. Genesis—Biography.
4. Patriarchs (Bible)—Biography.   I. Title.
BS580.A3A38   1993   222'.11092—dc20   92–42259 CIP

ISBN 0–8191–9027–6 (cloth : alk. paper)

Dedication: To my mother, my mother's mother, my mother's mother....unto Abraham.

Table of Contents:

Preface

PREFACE

Many of the ideas in this book have their roots in a Ph.D. Dissertation written over 15 years ago (Abraham: Psychology of a Spiritual Revolutionary and his Hebrew Chroniclers, Dept of Psychology, Yale 1977). It has taken me until I was myself approaching mid-life to revise it. In this interim, a son of Abram - Abramovitch - "vitch" is the slavic version of "son of" I too went off wandering, at times with my "sister" Ilana, a sister who everyone assumed was my wife. At times I wandered alone, arriving ultimately in the land promised to Abraham, still so full of the strife between his "children": Jewish newcomers and Palestinian oldtimers. If Abraham and indeed Genesis as a whole has a message for our times, it is, I feel, the promise, not of Land, but of the reconciliation of brother with brother. May Abraham, the father of so many, be yet a shield for us all and guide us, across the generations, showing us the pathways to peace.

So many people were helpful to me in the preparation of this work and I cannot mention them all, for their names are legion. Let me express my gratitude first of all to my wife, Iva Bader Abramovitch. To my teachers and mentors then at Yale: William James McGuire - who helped sustain me in the dark night of my soul; Daniel J. Levinson - who taught me what adult development meant long before I was ready to know and showed me what a mentor can be; the late Helen Block Lewis - with whom I was synchronistically reunited in the alleys of Jerusalem before her sudden death; Leonard W. Doob - who believed in me and shared his "wild ideas"; William Hallo - my reluctant guide to ancient near eastern history and texts; Robert Jay Lifton - who taught me the importance of death and the continuity of life and helped me heal my own broken connection; Rabbi Arnold Jacob Wolf - who showed me that even prophets can laugh.

For sustaining friendship and fellowship in New Haven: Gilda Outremont, Larry Katz, the Woodmont Wildcats and the folks at the Stonehouse.

To my "chavruta" (study partners) in Jerusalem who weekly share passions for Holy Scripture: Shlomi Naeh, George Savran, Eliezer Schwartz.

To my older brother, Lavy Yitzchak Abramovitch - who taught me about being firstborn/laterborn and suffered in my place.

To my other "brothers", Rabbi James E. Ponet, David Shulman, Raja Shehadeh: walking, dreaming, speaking, together and apart.

And finally, to my father, and the blessed memory of my mother, in whose memory this project was first conceived.

Jerusalem, January 1992
Hebrew Date. ירושלים, טבת התשנ״ב

PART ONE:
INTRODUCTION

The "Akeda" as a Dagger Overhead

A dagger above.
A child below.
An old father
making ready to slay his son...

Genesis 22:1-19 tells the story of the "akeda" עקדה, the binding of Isaac, as it is known in Hebrew tradition.

The story is like a dagger overhead: A religious anomaly, a horrible perversion. Scholars, commentators, theologians and interpreters have repeatedly tried to understand this moment in Biblical history as something other than what it is — the grossest violation of the human order, a father about to murder his son. For example, Augustine saw the "sacrifice of Isaac" as the clearest prefiguration of the sacrifice of Jesus in which another Father offers up his only Son. For Moslems, the sacrifice (usually attributed to the first promised son, Ishmael) is the ultimate test of faith, the proof of things unseen and the reality of the resurrection. For Jews, the story may justify the promises given so often to the patriarchs; it may prefigure (and explain) the pre-eminence of Jerusalem, identified with Mt. Moriah; it is the source of the notion of "ancestral merit", in which the deeds of the fathers are remembered to the good of their often undeserving descendants. It is almost certainly, as many rationalistic apologists try to argue, **not** a decisive act to end human sacrifice and replace it with animal offerings. Nowhere in the story is the issue addressed directly and human sacrifice overtly continued in the days of Jephtach, Menassheh, Mesha and covertly "unto this very day". Moreover, the entire episode, but especially Isaac's pivotal question, "Here are the firestone and the wood, but where is the sheep for the burnt offering?" (22:7), is based on the regular occurrence of animal sacrifice, the accepted means of communion in those days. Nor does Kierkegaard's fanciful if fascinating retelling of the three days' march do justice to the text: Who can believe that a "knight of faith" must at the fateful moment trick his son, saying he is Canaanite Idolator, so that Isaac will call out in the Name of his God? Since no sacrifice actually took place, the Hebrew name is the "akeda", the binding of Isaac. But in times of moral madness, genocide, it is all too tempting to cry, "the old man did not stay his hand", as Jewish victims of the Crusades, or battlefield offerings of the Great War declare in the following two poems:

> ... *He made haste, he pinned him down with his knee,*
> *He made his two arms strong.*
> *With steady hands he slaughtered him according to rite*
> *Full right was the slaughter*
>
> *Down upon him fell the resurrecting dew, and he revived.*
> *The father seized him then slaughtered him once more*
> *Scripture bear witness ! Well grounded is the fact:*
> *And the Lord called Abraham, even a second time from heaven.*
>
> *The ministering angels cried out, terrified:*
> *Even animal victims, were they ever slaughtered twice?...*

R. Ephraim of Bonn, 12th century in The Last Trial (Spiegel 1979)

> *...When lo! an angel called him out of heaven*
> *Saying, Lay not thy hand upon the lad,*
> *Neither do anything to him. Behold,*
> *A ram, caught in a thicket by its horns,*
> *Offer the Ram of Pride instead of him.*
> *But the old man would not so, but slew his son, -*
> *And half the seed of Europe, one by one*

Wilfred Owen (1931:122)

The story of the akeda, seen personally ("Could **I** really be ready to murder my son?", "Could **my** father really be ready to kill me?"; "What kind of a God would **want** such a "sacrifice"?"); taken seriously ("What was the akeda trying to say then? What, in heavens' name could it mean for us today?") is a horrible conundrum.

Abraham as a Psychiatric Case

Seen as an isolated event, the akeda is the work of a madman: Abraham as a psychiatric case. From this point of view, the akeda is the psychotic culmination of a severely disturbed personality. Like many people who believe "God" is talking to them, Abraham suffered from auditory and visual hallucinations. One may speak of bizarre sadistic and masochistic tendencies, frighteningly expressed in a "folie à deux", the self mutilation of himself and his adolescent son. Although there are narcissistic and antisocial aspects in "delusions of grandeur", his basic diagnosis is probably identity disorder aggravated by "multiple migrations".

As part of his grandiose delusional system he changes his name, his place of residence (at least ten times) and displays severe psychopathology in his interpersonal relation with his wife and sons. On two separate occasions he exhibits severe role confusion, not knowing whether he is a "brother" or a "husband"; signs of marital breakdown include psychogenic impotence and infertility, passivity, being dominated by his wife. Other sources of psychosocial stress include: sudden death of his eldest brother, chronic problem with authority ("antisocial" tendencies), bizarre ritualistic behavior, and childlessness.

The psychodymamic significance of the akeda as part of this psychiatric case report would stress his "Laius complex"[1] (Laius was Oedipus' father who on learning from an oracle that his son would kill him, sent the infant away to die from exposure). Such filicidal urges might be considered the effects of unresolved Oedipal competition with his father, displaced onto his own son-competitor, enacting on his son the experience of "castration" by a cruel and jealous father. An alternative explanation asserts that the father, envious of their youthful prowess and future, expresses murderous jealous rage of the old toward the young. Like many psychotic parents who murder their children, Abraham felt "commanded" to do so.

Such a "Godless" view of Abraham, as a psychiatric case, tells us little about Abraham, Father of Believers and Nations, or the unfolding of his spiritual revolution. It is true that many of the things Abraham and Sarah did must have seemed strange, or bizarre, even to themselves. But such a clinical "outsiders" perspective does not allow us to see in to Abraham's achievement, only his distress.

Such a reductionistic view of his "craziness" serves as a reminder of the spiritual poverty of most contemporary psychiatry. Hiding behind bizarre symptoms and personality disorders, there are people who are yearning, like Abraham, to find a Way.

The Text of Genesis 22 clearly shows us that the akeda is not to be interpreted in isolation but in some narrative, life-historical sequence.[2] Unlike the initial call

(12:1) from Haran "to the land that I will show you", the akeda story begins with the Biblical phrase "Some time afterward" or more literally in the King James translation, "And it came to pass after these things. ..": "Which things?" the attentive reader is impelled to ask. The answer to this question occupies this book. What is the significance of the akeda within the adult development/life cycle of Abraham? What went before, which allows the reader to understand Abraham neither a madman, nor a bloody-minded idealist willing to kill for his "divine" ideals; not the compliant killer or the archetypal child abuser, but rather "The First Father"?

Hebrew Text and English Translation

In this work, I have used the Hebrew text as the basis of my study, and in the course of the work I shall refer to the Hebrew Text as needed. I have chosen the new Jewish Publication Society translation as my main English version and when not otherwise indicated it is usually the translation given. This translation is perhaps the most widely accepted English version used by Jews in the English-speaking world. In trying to bridge "author-oriented" and "audience-oriented" concerns (e.g. by the use of footnotes), it often strays too far from the original for our purposes. The King James version, for all its limitations, provides a more literal counterpoint, and on occasion I have prefered the Catholic Jerusalem Bible (based on the French original "La Bible de Jerusalem"). I did also consult Speiser's Anchor Bible version of Genesis and Everett Fox's English Rendition of the German language Buber-Rosenszweig Translation of the Bible. As J.P.S. version acknowledges, in many Biblical passages the meaning of the Hebrew is uncertain; cf. 2:12; 3:5; 4:7; 6:2; 6:3; 14:14; 15:2; 16;13; 17:1; 22:14; 24:63; 25:22 etc, When my own translation differs from one of the standard renditions, I have indicated so in the text. Biblical reference, unless otherwise indicated, refers to passages in Genesis.

Outline of The Life of Abraham

The details of Abraham's life in Genesis may be briefly summarized. He is born Abram, son of Terah, in the city state of Ur, Southern Mesopotamia. No information about his mother, birth, childhood or youth is given. The only facts of his early adult life concern the death of a brother and a childless marriage. At some point, his father, Terah, decides to take the entire family across the Fertile Crescent to Canaan, but only manages to get halfway, to Northen Mesopotamia, where he later dies.

Abram takes his own entourage, including the son of his dead brother, and completes his father's journey in response to an inner voice. Famine soon forces him out of the "promised land" and into Egypt, where his wife, posing as his sister, is taken into Pharaoh's harem. Abram prospers but when the deception is exposed, he and his wife are deported. Returning to Caanan he separates from his nephew, who abandons the pure pastoral for the corrupting urban life. Abram then is forced to rescue Lot when the later is captured by the invading Mesopotamian army and receives social and political recognition from the local rulers after his victory. This incident is followed by a vision and new relation with his Lord, who promises that he **will** have children of his own but that his descendants will undergo generations of hardship and great suffering in exile, returning only in the 4th generation, to receive the Land. These promises are affirmed by an unusual ritual sacrifice, and Abram himself is promised a peaceful old age.

As seeming fulfilment of these promises, Abram does have a son by his wife's handmaid, Hagar. This arrangement causes much tension between Abram and his wife, and Hagar even tries to flee the encampment. Again nothing is told about this son's childhood or youth, but 13 years later Abram receives another revelation. He is told to circumcize all males in his camp, to change his name to Abraham (and his wife's to Sarah). He also learns, to his own incredulous laughter that the old couple will have a son together who will be their real heir.

At this point, Abraham learns about the imminent destruction of Sodom and Gomorrah. Using priciples of universal justice and saving grace of the just, Abraham bargains with God in a vain attempt to save the cities. After the cities are destroyed, Abraham moves again, this time to Gerar, a city-state in the south of the country.

Once again Sarah, posing as sister, is abducted by the local king, but before she is dishonored her true identity is revealed to the king in a dream. In compensation, Abraham is given rights of residence and money. Moreover, he is for the first time called a "prophet" and prays for the health of the women of the royal household. Later that year, a second son is born to Abraham whose name, Isaac, derives from the verbal root for "laughter".

At Isaac's weaning feast Sarah forces Abraham to expel the handmaid Hagar and her son Ishmael. As Abraham's social standing grows, he is sought out by the local king to arrange a formal peace treaty, and Abraham uses this opportunity to settle long-standing grievances over water rights.

"Some time later" he receives a final call to offer up his only remaining son as a whole burnt offering. Without questioning such an immoral command, he sets out, with Isaac and two servants.

After three days he sees the site selected for the human sacrifice and goes up alone with Isaac. At the very last moment, as Abraham raises his dagger to slay his son, a heavenly messenger stops him and reveals that it was only a test. Promises made earlier concerning land, progeny and destiny are repeated.

At the death of his wife, Abraham acquires a burial cave to serve as the family sepulcher and then arranges a marriage for his son Issac with kinsmen from Mesopotamia. He himself takes another wife, Keturah, by whom he has six more sons, but Issac remains his chief heir. In old age, "blessed in all things", he dies and is buried by his two sons.

"Crisis of Generativity"

Such are the bare facts. But these "facts" do not give the sense of Abraham's role as the prototypical "spiritual revolutionary". Detailed examination of his life, I claim, will not only give insight into his teachings but also into the psychological dilemmas which such innovators face.

Abraham is spiritual in that he confronts the Ultimate Concerns: the meaning of life, death, evil, divine justice; how living with God entails doing "what is right and just" with one's fellows. In terms of moral development, Abraham represents a Biblical highpoint, integrating a tribal particularism with a universal morality. But Abraham is also very much a revolutionary in that he made a decisive break with his past, formulating a new collective identity for his descendant-disciples.

In founding this new order, he experienced the persistent conflict between radical innovation and the search for security. Such tensions, I will argue, are an inherent paradox in the life of any revolutionary, or in any situation which pits innovation against tradition. Innovators, whether spiritual or otherwise, inevitably must face a "crisis of generativity", of how to pass on the tradition of revolution/innovation to the next generation. The success in resolving such a generativity crisis will often determine the moral success and survival of the revolutionary project.

Abraham's mission is often spoke of as a story of faith, or blind obedience. I believe it is about the search for continuity.

Three Approaches to the Story of Abraham

In this study of Abraham I have tried to combine three distinct approaches: Biblical studies, cultural anthropology and life-cycle psychology. From Biblical studies, I apply a "close reading" of the Hebrew Text of Genesis 11:26-25:12. Drawing on principles of cultural anthropology, I treat the same Text as an ethnographic document, fairly accurately reflecting the cultural practices, kinship pattern, ecology, rituals etc. of Abraham and his tribe. From life-cycle psychology, I draw on the recent developments in theory of adult development, which asserts that adulthood has a sequence of age-based stages or seasons, each with its own psychological tasks and emotional climate. Combining all three approaches, I therefore treat the narrative account of the story of Abraham as a "life history".[3]

Adult development shares with Biblical studies a concern for narrative continuity. Much of Old Testament Narrative concerns the formation, disruption and subsequent reaffirmation of the ongoing relationship between the God of Israel and His people. Within Genesis, the Patriarchal narratives, the story of Abraham, his children, grandchildren and greatgrandchildren, serve as a bridge across an historical disjunction: linking a mythic past of the first eleven chapters to a collective tribal future in Exodus and after. For God the Creator, the selection of Abraham and his family represents a new attempt to secure an ongoing relationship with mankind, after having given up on humanity as a whole. If Abraham's descendant-disciples accept his teachings, then they will be God's vehicle to bring blessing "on all the families of the earth".

Likewise in mid-life, a man's story may break down. He often loses his way within his life story. His painful task is to try to form a new narrative, out of his fragments. He must form a new "life structure" and create a new story, one he can tell others, and live with himself. Such a "reconstructed" life story is necessarily a fiction, imposing retrospective order on the chaos of possibilities. But when such stories do contain one's inner truth, then they grant one a transcendant sense of continuity.

Abram's story is such a quest. It is a spiritual voyage very different from the heroic pattern of youth, exemplified and parodied by another middle age hero, Don Quixote. There, the hero sets out to prove himself, by performing feats of bravery, and thereby winning the hand of his beloved. The "hero myth" of a mid-life quest has a rather different rhythm. In keeping with the transition from the first to the second half of life, it is a darker, more inward looking, spiritual adventure; one that borders on madness. It may require abandoning all - family, friends, one's place in society, all that one has so meticulously built up in the first half of life. It may be, as it was for Odysseus, a restless, tragic searching for a lost home, for one's place in the universe.

Mid-life is the time when a young man begins to become old; when he begins to realize that his own death will be inevitable. It is an era when issues of generativity, continuity and creativity come to the fore along with their stark contrasts: stagnation, broken connections, being "cut off". Abram's middle-age quest begins with such a crisis of generativity: he has no sons. And in his culture, being without children means being "cut off". His search for offspring leads him into a quest for spiritual generativity, which transforms him from a sonless son, into The First Father.

"No book has attracted the attention of modern Biblical scholarship more than Genesis" (Rendsburg 1986:1).

Genesis 12-25 as a Life History

Which Abraham?

There has been a recent rediscovery of the Biblical text by social and human scientists. Beside the more traditional disciplines of Biblical studies (philology, archeology, ancient Near Eastern texts and parallels, theology etc.) aspects of Biblical life have been studied by: political scientists (Wildavsky 1984; Rosenberg 1986), game theorist (Brams 1980), structural anthropologists (Leach 1969; Leach & Aycock 1983; Greenwood 1985; Eilberg-Schwartz 1990), ethnographers (Pitt-Rivers I978; Rogerson 1979; Lang 1985) students of kinship and geneology (Wilson 1975, 1977; Andriolo 1973, 1981; Donaldson 1981; Oden 1983; Prewitt 1981); sociologists (Gottwald 1979; Wilson 1984; Malina 1984; Rodd 1981); folklore theorists (Graves & Patai 1964; Niditch 1987; Dundes 1984) feminists (Fewell 1987; Collins 1985; Russell 1985; Stone 1976; Sacks 1982;) psychologists (Bakan 1971, 1979), psychoanalysts (Zeligs 1974 ;Beck 1968; Shoham l976; Wellisch 1954; Reik 1961) and a host of literary critics (Fokkelman 1971; Bar Efrat 1979; Alter 1981; Gros Louis 1982; Fishbane 1983; Berlin 1983; McKinght 1985; Sternberg 1985; Frye 1982; Bloom 1986; Gottcent 1986; McConnell 1986; Preminger & Greenstein 1986; Alter & Kermode 1987).

Ironically, these new literary and sociological approaches are flourishing at a time when the more traditional use of archeology, and ancient Near Eastern parallels has come under attack (Van Seters 1975; Thompson 1974; Millard & Wiseman 1980; Hunter 1986). No longer is it possible to assert that the patriarchal narratives correspond uniquely to life in Second Millenium BCE nor indeed that it may ever be possible to uncover the "historical Abraham". Instead, we are left with "the stories themselves" (Thompson 1987), "a world that is in the texts themselves and only in those texts" (p.198). Indeed, this is only right, since it is the men and women who are presented via the text who are important. The "Abraham of Believers" is the

Abraham revealed in Genesis 12-25, not his hypothetical historical counterpart who almost certainly left no written records or identifiable artifacts. Following Cassuto, Fishbane, Rendsburg and Rosenberg, critics of the documentary hypothesis, and like simple believers, I propose to treat the text as a whole. I do not reject the notion that the present text may be made up of various traditions, layers, sources, editings and re-editings.[3] Rather I argue, along with much recent critical opinion, that there is a literary and psychological unity in the presentation of the Bible, even in the apparently disorganized "anthology of Abraham" stories.

The focus of this study is not a "historical Abraham" who might be reconstructed from the text, nor is it the history of the text whose "conclusions that have been reached are far from unanimous and the foundations on which this literary criticism has been based have been called into question again and again" (De Vaux 1978:161). The Biblical Text of Genesis was certainly written down many generations after Abraham might have lived[4] - e.g, internal evidence of Gen 14 date it after the move of the tribe of Dan to the north in the period of the Judges. Scholars note anachronistic references to Ur of the Chaldees and, possibly, camels and texts of historical-religious material are inevitably adapted to the needs of the chronicler and audience at certain psychohistorical moments (Erikson 1968).

Instead I take Abraham as he appears in the present redacted text (Rendsburg 1986) who is the Abraham for believers. This Abraham is at once the founding ancestor for the tribes of Israel, the one to whom the Promises were first made (Westermann 1980). He is also "father of many nations" - Ishmaelites, all his descendants by his third wife, Keturah (25:1-4) and indirectly Sparta (I Mac 13:20), and Edom (36:1). In this way he emerges not only in a tribal identity but as a universal figure of faith, the first prophet, the defender of mankind and universal justice: "Shall not the Judge of all earth deal justly?" (18:25). In his ongoing relationship with the divine, he initiates a new kind of relationship with God, one based on contractual reciprocity (**brit**) which is both everlasting **and** conditional on the moral behavior of his descendants (18:19). This is, I feel, the crux of the spiritual revolution which made him into "avraham avinu", "our father Abraham" for the Jews, "Father Abraham" for Christians and "el-khalil", the friend of Allah, for Moslems. One could say without exaggeration that this Abraham, is one of the most influential persons in the spiritual history of humankind.

"Unlike symptoms, which, one hopes, succumb to the power of good interpretation, great myths and works of art seem to thrive on interpretation. With it, they survive and flourish, and gain significance. Without it, they perish. Thus to participate in the tradition of interpreting... is to preserve that very tradition." (Spitz, 1988:377)

"Dor dor vedorshav"[5]:
Each Generation / Its own Interpretation

The Hebrew maxim, דור דור ודורשיו "dor dor vedorshav" asserts that each generation needs its own interpreters. Shifting and resifting, "turning it over and over", to use a Rabbinic phrase, is a hermeneutic necessity for each generation. Such a "generational" or life cycle approach to Scripture implicitly denies (despite official claims to the contrary) that there can be fixed, lasting understanding of the Biblical Text. Instead, each historical community (and today, perhaps, each individual) must seek to discover the links between the Text and the realities of their time; relating, for example, the life histories of the Patriarchs, the Fathers to their own life story and that of their generation. Indeed, within an individual's life cycle, the same stories may take on radically different significance - the story of David may mean something very different to a young, middle-aged or old person. The search for understanding, as Erikson argued in the"Psychology of Chronicler", must be understood in terms of the life cycle of the community, as well as the life cycle of the individual chronicler.

We inherit along with religion the interpretations of former generations. Often, the hermeneutics of the past may still hold true for the next, inheritor/successor generation. But it may not. Then the text must be "turned over", re-approached, and re-discovered and so as to be revitalized. But when this process of "textual revitalization" does not occur, the words become "dead letters", condemned to irrelevance and forgotten. In that case, the text is no longer the vehicle of "symbolic immortality" (Lifton 1979) or intergenerational communication.

My interpretation of Abraham is therefore definitely not definitive. It does represent an attempt to rescue Abraham as a "living presence" for believer and sceptic alike. It is a sort of modern "midrash", a psychological, anthropologically informed commentary on the man revealed by the Biblical Narrative: One "reading" of his life history. Although I am trained in analytic psychology, I have not attempted to psychoanalyze Abraham (cf. Wellisch 1954; Reik 1961; Zeligs 1974; Beck 1968; Shoham 1976), since the relevant information about his early life is unknown. There is, for example, no mention in Scripture of his mother; no childhood[6] nor anything approaching free associations of his inner life, feelings and fantasies. Instead I use life cycle psychology, cultural anthropology and such to understand Abraham's life course and his spiritual odyssey in terms which make contemporary sense. For our purposes, we shall treat the Biblical text as something other than what it was intended, viz. as a "personal document" revealing fairly accurately the adult life course of the man who was becoming Abraham, the first Patriarch.

Hebrew Text/English Translation:

A few peculiarites of the Hebrew text require mentioning. In a few places, a speech or part of a sentence, seems to have been deliberately deleted. The clearest example is when Cain lures Abel into the field. The J.P.S. version gives a clear sense of the original: "And Cain said to his brother Abel...and when they were in the field, Cain set upon his brother Abel and killed him" (4:8); and in a note adds "Ancient versions, including the Targum, read "Come let us go into the field". And Why? Why was Cain's speech deliberately suppressed or deleted? A midrash suggests the deletion protects the purity of speech and the possibility of dialogue, namely, so as not to taint the language of brothers with the hidden suggestion of Cain. Otherwise, whenever one might hear "Come let us go into the field", he would immediately, even if unconsciously, feel "murder"! Similarly, there appears to be some minor ellipsis in Chapter 18 esp. v. 22 which make it unclear whether Abraham was standing before the Lord, before His unseen presence or in the guise of one of the messengers. Likewise, Avimelech's reply to God in the dream (20:4) is obscure, possibly the result of a scribal error - however the sense seems clear: "O Lord, will you slay people even though innocent?" (J.P.S.) or more simply "My Lord, would you kill innocent people, too?" (Jerusalem Bible) or trying to incorporate the difficult original, "Lord, wilt thou slay also a righteous nation?" (King James).

Hebrew manuscripts, like the ritually prescribed Torah scroll, are written only with consonants. Oral tradition preserved how the text was to be read since "vowel sounds were transmitted by memory from teacher to pupil. This method was not difficult while Hebrew was a spoken language, but variants in traditions of how to pronounce the consonantal text arose as the Jews were scattered far and wide and different native languages became their means of speech" (Livingston 1987:209). Beginning in the 7th century C.E. various attempts were made to introduce vowel and accent markings, and the most widely accepted version derives from the "Masoretes" who placed marginal notes on the page of the text, known as "Masora". The Masoretes, flourished in Tiberias, on the west bank of the Sea of Galilee in the 8th and 9th century, and devised a system of marking called "points" made up of seven vowel signs and 32 accent marks, which guide the ritual chanting of the Biblical Text.

On the other hand, the oldest complete versions of the Old Testament are only about a thousand years old e.g. Allepo Codex; Codex Leningradensis (1008 C.E.). Manuscript translations of Hebrew into Greek (LXX, or Septuagint), Aramaic (Targum), Syriac (Peshitta) or Latin (Vulgate), as well as the Samaritan Pentateuch, often exist in much older versions. In addition, the Dead Sea Scrolls, which are some of the oldest versions of many Biblical texts, include a fascinating supplement to Genesis, known as Genesis Aprocryphon (Avigad & Yaddin 1956)[7]. I have almost always followed the massoretic pointing of the Hebrew text, but it must be noted that translations and much Rabbinic discourse is based on alternative vocalization of the written consonants. A few examples may suffice.

In Genesis 15:11, it is written birds of prey came down upon the carcasses of the severed animals of the so-called "sacrifice between the pieces". Modern translations following the Masoretes translate the end of the passage: "And Abram drove them away". The Septuagint (LXX), however translates the same passage, based on a differing vocalization of the root "ישב" "YSB" as "and he sat down with them" (Brenton 1851). There is a great difference between sitting down with the eagles or chasing them away (cf. Weinfeld et. al. 1982). Likewise, much of the creative imagination of Rabbinic interpretations is based on deliberate "misreading" of known "spoken text". Thus the term אור כשדים "Ur Kasdim", usually understood as "Ur of the Chaldeans" אוּר, could alternatively be read as "Or" of the Chaldeans i.e. the "light" or "fire" of the Chaldeans. This misreading is the basis for a Rabbinic tradition that Abram, like Daniel 3-4, survived torture in a fiery furnace and the death of his brother, Haran, an impulsive believer, resulted from him impetuously leaping into the flames after Abram.

" the Lord God formed man from the
dust of the earth..." (2:7)

A Note on Translation

No English translation can convey the verbal sequence and word play of the Hebrew Biblical Text. To give one outstanding example, the passage which describes the creation of man (2:7) reads: "and God formed man (**ha-adam**) from the dust of the earth (**ha-adama**)." In a language built on verbal roots, obligatory gender, man is the masculine form of the feminine earth, אדם/אדמה **adam/adama**. But within the word adam, hides another term, דם **dam** (blood) which completes the verbal sequece; **dam, adam, adama**. דם, אדם, אדמה

This verbal sequence forms the basis of much Biblical poetry, e.g.

"Whoever sheds the blood (dam)
of man (ha-adam),
By man (ba-adam) shall his blood (dam-o) be shed
For in his image
Did God make man. (9:6).

and perhaps much of an implicit narrative theology. God as "Father" made man (adam) from Earth, the "mother" i.e. The Lord God is progenitor with earth ("adama") of man ("adam"), or as the Hebrew reveals "adam" is the son of "adama". Eve (Hebrew: חוה "Chava"), the mother of mankind is likewise made by the holy spirit out of Adam's rib - and here too there is a word play rib צלע ("tsela") and essense or image צלם ("tselem"); but more, the Hebrew word עצם "etsem" serves for both "bone" and "essence", another theological pun which evades even the more literal or "author-oriented" translation (Greenstein 1983):

This one at last
Is bone of my bone
And flesh of my flesh.
This one shall be called Woman ("ishsha")
For from man ("ish") was she taken. (2:23)

Hebrew word play is also found in personal and place names. Names in the ancient Near East were not mere labels or means of identification, rather "the name of a man was intimately involved with the very essense of his being and inextricably intertwined with his personality" (Sarna 1966:129). God creates by naming: "Let there be light" and there was light. (1:3); Man orders his world by naming the animals, his first act in the image of God (2:19-20). Conversely, anonymity is the equivalent of non-being. Thus, to "cut off the name" means to end existence, to annihilate, and in Egypt, with its death-centered religion, the way to bring an end to the continued existence of a deceased person in the afterlife was by effacing his name from his tomb" (Sarna 1966:130). The worst fate is for a person's name to be blotted out (cf. Deut 25:6; Gen. 38). Names carry "multivocal" significance. Sometimes two or three differing versions are offered: cf. the three etymologies of Beersheva as "well of the oath" and "well of the seven" or "well of harassment" (21:22-34, 26:33), double naming of Ishmael ישמעאל ("God heeds" or "God has heard" or perhaps "God will hear") by Hagar and later by Abraham (Gen 17:11; 17:15); likewise Isaac, in Hebrew, יצחק "Yitzchak" means "he laughed" recalling that both Abraham and Sarah had laughed when told that a son would be born to them (cf. 17:17;18:12), and the theme of laughter runs through Isaac's early life. At his weaning feast Sarah sings, "God has brought me laughter; everyone who hears will laugh with me" (21:6).

The same verbal root "laugh" or "play" is used in the verse "Sarah saw the son whom Hagar the Egyptian had borne to Abraham playing (misacheik)" (21:9) and the same word, "Misakheik" is used with a clear sexual connation when Avimelech catches Isaac and Rebekah "fondling" or "sporting" (26:8). Again the Hebrew texts sets up the verbal sequence יצחק - מצחק "yitzchak" - "misakheik": laughing-Isaac-playing-fondling all centered on the same verbal root "yitzchak". Such word play[8] is central to the narrative technique of the Hebrew Text.

The dilemma of how best to translate[9] will remain:

So long as the earth endures (8:22)

CHAPTER TWO:
ABRAHAM IN CONTEXT

In this chapter, I try to place the Biblical account of the life of Abraham and his family in context.

First, I discuss the role this family history plays within the literary-theological structure of the Book of Genesis, as a bridge between a mythological past (chapters 1-11) and a collective future as a People (Exodus and beyond).

Second, I examine the adult development of Abraham himself, within the structure of the life cycle, focusing especially on Daniel Levinson's theory of adult development as expounded in his well-known book, "The Seasons of a Man's Life".

Third, I suggest how Biblical conceptions of biography, the course of a life, differ significantly from some contemporary notions.

The Literary Structure Of The Book Of Genesis

The book of Genesis is divided into four major sections. The first eleven chapters describe primeval history of mankind; Chapters 12-25 tell the life history of Abraham and his family; the next 11 chapters recount the early life of Jacob, as well as a few details of his father Isaac and brother Esau; the rest of Genesis (37-50) tells the story of Joseph and his brothers, which is more akin to a short novel or novella than the previous patriarchal family histories. The primeval history recounts the creation of the universe and the early history of humankind. Of all the Bible, it is the section which is closest to myth. The image of God presented is of a passionate Creator, capable of pride and regrets, destructive impulses but also elegant stratagems. Even in these early chapters, God appears, to use Heschel's beautiful phrase, "God in search of man", one with whom He can engage in an ongoing dialogue and who by righteousness will make His name great.

The main stories in the primeval saga, the Garden, the Fratricide, the Flood, the curse on Canaan, and the Tower of Babel describe the moral degeneration of humanity. The trajectory of decline contrasts the ideal of pastoralist-gatherer society with the evils of agrarian-urban environment. Likewise there is the divine concern that mankind will try to supplant the Creater (3:22; 11:4) and bring about moral and cosmic chaos (6:1-5; 8:21-22). God, the Spiritual Father (and Mother), is able to inflict ruthless punishment, but ultimately God places limits on his own destructiveness by his rainbow covenant with Noah (9:8-17).

The Creation of mankind by a single Creator (in both accounts of creation 1:27; 2:7-25) projects a worldview of the essential unity of humankind. As such, it rejects the more typical ethnocentric perspective (or "pseudospeciation") in which "my people" are seen as human, while other peoples or tribes are classed as some lesser category of being. The God of Abraham is the God of All peoples of the Earth, a universal Divinity, acting through a paticular nation.

Another major element in the primeval saga, and indeed the entire Bible, is the list of תולדות "toledot", usually translated as "descendants of" or "line" or even "story of". The "toledot" are geneological descriptions of the dispersion of humanity in lineal descent. These genealogies served, as they do for many peoples, as a cognitive and ontological map. They describe (from the perspective of Israelite culture) the relation among nations, how close or remote their sense of kinship: at the same time they describe a moral ordering of the taintedness of certain tribes in contrast with the pure descent of the Hebrews. Thus, all Semites share a common ancestor Shem, who is the focus for their sense of kinship; while the descendants of Canaan, the indigenous inhabitants of the promised land, were an accursed people, condemned by Noah to inferior social status (9:25). An extension of this moral and cognitive map occurs in the story of Abraham, discussed below.

The transition from the primeval saga to the patriarchal narratives involves a shift from concern with humanity as a whole to that of one clan. Over and against the disenchantment with humanity comes the story of Abraham, a single individual through which God may speak to all the nations of the earth. Michael Fishbane, a sensitive student of Biblical "Text and Texture" has written:

> *Abram is like Noah, a new Adam and a renewal of human life in history. In a sense the entire primeval cycle is a prologue to him and his toledot. He is the new steward and hope "east of Eden". It is therefore striking, but, by no means unexpected, that God's promises to him at the beginning of the patriarchal cycle (12:1-3) reverse the Curses of Eden...*
>
> *Exile, curse and the pain of childbirth "east of Eden" (cf. Genesis 3) now yield the hope of a new land and ingathering of divine blessing, and of fertile generation...The gloom of the preceding chapters is somewhat abated, and the possibility of earthly existence with God is renewed. With Abram and his faithful response to God's presence, the primeval cycle is brought to a close, and the cycle of the fathers begins.*

Fishbane 1979:39

The history of Abraham begins in mid-life. In contrast, the stories concerning

Jacob center mostly on early life - his birth, rivalry and marriage - and effectively ends with the simultaneous birth of Benjamin and death of his beloved Rachel. The transitional chapter 36 gives toledot of Esau, which sets apart the Jacob narratives from the Joseph story.

The story of Joseph and his brothers are a bridge between the patriarchal narratives and the Exodus to follow. The theme of the reconciliation of brothers also serves as an underlying unity to the entire book of Genesis. (Dahlberg 1982)[10]. Human history, which is from the beginning the history of a family, begins with the bitter jealous rivalry of brothers. The result is the first murder, which in the narrated theology of Genesis suggests that all murder is fratricide. The theme of fraternal rivalry recurs among Noah's, Abraham's, Isaac's, Jacob's and even Joseph's sons. Often as in the case of Jacob, (and possibly Isaac, and even God as the primal Spiritual Father) the murderous rivalry is the result of a father's favoritism. Thus the exile of Joseph in Egypt results from paternal preference and his own dreamy grandiosity/pride. As with Cain and Abel, or Jacob and Esau, brother is set against brother. The final divinely inspired union of brothers ("So, it was not you who sent me here, but God" 45:8), sets the theme of redemption through the reuniting of brothers. The same redemptive process is carried over to Exodus when the younger brother Moses returns to his elder brother Aaron, and together, they bring about God's miracle, the redemption of Israel.

In this way, Genesis sets the stage for what is to come. Dahlberg in his essay "The Unity of Genesis" has caught this notion in saying:

...One might compare the book of Genesis as a whole to an orchestral overture to a dramatic opera; an introduction, yes, but also a work of art complete in itself - a sort of overview of what is to take place, a survey in prospect of all the great themes. God already does in Genesis what he will do again in the deliverance from Egypt. Readers faced in life with the experience of Exodus can "take heart", so to speak, from Genesis.

Dahlberg 1982:132-3

In contrast to the stories of Jacob and Joseph, the text concerning Abraham is episodic, an "anthology of stories" about the First Father. Some scholars have felt that the narrative is so fragmented that one scholar has asked "Is there a story of Abraham?" (Rosenberg 1986). Recent scholarship, however, following the suggestion of the great Italian-Jewish Biblical scholar Umberto Cassuto, and more recent analyses of Fishbane, have shown that the Abraham stories, as indeed all of Genesis, has a sophisticated if subtle literary format (Rendsberg 1986; Rosenberg 1986; Coats 1983). The stories which appear separate episodes are arranged in

mirror-like parallels, ABCDE E'D'C'B'A".[11] A number of items in the main texts of
the Abraham cycle (Genesis 11:26-Genesis 22:24) are set out and then repeated in
reverse order, back to front, so that it appears as a "chiastic parallel":
ABCDEE'D'C'B'A'. In the first part of the narrative (11:27-16:16) the hero is
known as Abram, while in the mirror part (17:1-22:24), he is known as Abraham.
The entire cycle begins and ends with geneological framework which, as we have
seen, provides the narrative frame for the story. The story proper begins with
leaving Haran and ends with news and later reconciliation with his brother's family
in Haran, through parallel cousin marriage alliance. The initial physical odyssey of
wandering is matched in literary phrasing with the final spiritual Odyssey at Moriah;
early altar building and promises are matched by later altars and promises. The first
wife/sister episode (12:10-20) is matched by a second such affair (20:1-18), and
even the border argreement with Lot (13:1-13) may find its parallel in the treaty with
Abimelech (21:22-34). The Sodom episode and rescue of Lot is exactly reiterated in
18:1-19:38.

The parallels are almost exact and suggest it is not a "crude disjointed tale" in
which almost any episode may be omitted without seriously impairing the unity."[12]

The literary impact of such parallelism, as Alter and others have argued, is the
implied contrast between the first and second version. Robert Alter, in his book on:
The Art of Biblical Poetry, quotes the Russian Formalist critic Viktor Shlovsky,

*"The perception of disharmony in a harmonious context is important in
parallelism. The purpose of parallelism, like the general purpose of imagery,
is to transfer the usual perception of an object into the sphere of a new
perception - that is, to make a unique semantic modification"*

(Alter 1985:10)

The clearest "semantic modification" noted by many Hebrew Biblical
commentators and recent literary critics contrasts the initial call, which was full of
promises and free of obligations, with the call to the akeda, which was full of
obligations and free of promises. Indeed it contradicts all that was promised.

The parallelism of chapters 12-22 divide up the cycle of Abraham into his
mid-life period, which is the time of his seven epiphanies with God and a later
period of winding up affairs or final reconciliation(23-25). From a theological
point of view, one might ask why Biblical narrative devotes so much attention on
these seemingly purely domestic and mundane matters (burial of Sarah, arranging
marriage for son Isaac, marriage to third wife, Keturah and fate of her children) in
which God plays no part. The point, which is central to my argument, is that the
text in Genesis gives us a life history of Abraham which accounts for its seemingly

episodic character. In contrast, the Joseph narratives constitute what might be characterized as a "life story", focused on a single reconstructed unifying theme within the life history. No such "novelistic" unity is imposed on Abraham's life and his life story is only implicit. The inclusions of the late adulthood details are important events in his life history, even if his "affair" with God ends with the akeda. These events provide a picture of a successful life and a "good death". As such, Chapters 23-25 present the conclusion of a life, and thus the Biblical model of successful aging[13].

"Biblical Years" as Relative Indicators of the Life-Cycle

There is a second literary device which holds the stories of Abraham together, namely, that throughout the text his age is reported. He is 75 when he leaves Haran; 86 when Hagar bore him Ishmael; 99 when he circumcised "the flesh of his foreskin and that of his son, Ishmael"; 100 when Yitzchak was born; Sarah dies at 123 and Abraham still older arranges for Yitzchak's marriage to his kin in Mesopotamia, and later dies at 175. Significantly, his age (and therefore the age of Yitzchak) at the akeda seems deliberately left vague. Such concern with age of marker events is unprecedented in Scripture.

A number of Biblical scholars have argued that biblical numbers are "schematized and rhetorical rather than literal". Cassuto discovered that the ages of the three patriarchs may be expressed as follows:

Abraham	$175 - 7 \times 5^2$
Isaac	$180 - 5 \times 6^2$
Jacob	$147 - 3 \times 7^2$

an arrangement of ascending and descending factors related to ancient Babylonian and Egyptian number systems. Other number parallels also reveal the metaphorical use of Biblical years: Abram is 75 years with his father and 75 years with his son Isaac, as a father; 100 years in Canaan while he is 100 years old at the birth of Isaac (cf. similar analogies for Jacob and Joseph (Sarna 1966)).

Even the number 318, the number of men Abram leads into battle (14:14), appears to have special significance, as it appears on the Egyptian scarab of Amenhotep II, and in Homer as the number of the dead in battle (Gevirtz 1969).

What are we to make of Abraham's 175 years? Such a life span seems well beyond even the most inflated claims of contemporary long lived individuals, who do not seem to go beyond the traditional 120. Within Genesis, however, there is a trend of decreasing life span in Biblical Years as the text moves from the mythic environment of primeval saga to the more historical context of the exile in Egypt. Thus, Joseph is said to live 110 Biblical years. Physical anthropologists and archeologists, moreover, have argued that "early man" in Palestine during the Bronze Age lived much shorter lives than people today, so it is improbable that these lifespans can be taken literally.

My conjecture, is that in the case of Abraham, the chronology and life span are to be taken as "relative" indicators of his location within the life cycle. His life span of 175 Biblical years is roughly double the contemporary one. Applying this ratio to the other dates (2 Biblical Years = 1 contemporary year), we can see his life in perspective of theories of the life cycle (Erikson 1963) and adult development (Levinson 1977; Gould 1976).

The use of Biblical years as relative indicators of life cycle status allow us to say that Abraham at 75, the time of his first call, corresponds to a contemporary 37.5, the time Jung associated with "mid life". The birth of Ishmael at 86 would place him in his early forties. Circumcision and the birth of Isaac would occur in his fiftieth year. Sarah's death would find him in his late sixties or early seventies and his death would correspond to a contemporary eighty-seven. Such relative indicators could apply to his father Terah as well. In the seven previous generations the only age given is the age of the father upon the birth of his son, which was the main marker event in man's life. In all these generations, from Arpachshad to Nahor, paternity arrived when a man was about 30 Biblical Years (The mean is 31.4; the medium and mode are 30). Terah was 70 when he had sons born to him. In relative terms, the Text is telling us that Terah, like Abraham after him, suffered from "delayed Paternity".

Note that I am not suggesting that relative indicators of life cycle can be applied, for example, to the lifespans of the seven generations before Terah. These enormous ages like the antediluvian chronology, appear symbolic indicators of a "mythic" lifetime, incommensurate with our own.

Abraham's period of creative spiritual development the time of his seven epiphanies with God, extends from the biblical age of 75 until the akeda. In modern life cycle terms his spiritual flourishing takes place in middle adulthood, roughly from late thirties to late fifties to early sixties. This period, according to Erikson, has as its basic concern issues of "generativity versus stagnation". "Generativity is primarily the interest in establishing and guiding the next generation." (Erikson 1980:103) Generation is certainly the major concern of Abraham, who begins mid-life with the biological mode of generativity blocked, and so "cut off" from his generations. Indeed, one may say that it is a crisis of generativity, with its concurrent threat of stagnation and stasis which sparks the "mid-life crisis" involved in the call to leave Haran "to the place I shall show you".

The theme of rootlessness versus continuity is a major dimension of adult development. Jung spoke of the first and second halves of life, divided by an ever increasing awareness of lengthening shadows of death. Erikson, who put forward an influential conception of the life cycle, described the central task of middle adulthood as a dialectic between generativity, the feeling of being part of an ongoing vital process of generation in both senses of the word, versus stagnation, a sense of being stuck, static, immobile, unable to move or to create. Lifton's conception of death and the continuity of life put forward the recurring search for continuity and symbolic immortality, in deed or imagination, as the central form of development of the psyche of man in society. The loss and regaining of continuity is thus a central task of adult development, and it is against such context that we shall examine the life of Abraham as revealed in Biblical Text.

Levinson's Concept of Adult Development as Changing Life Structure

In this study of Abraham's adult development, I rely on Daniel J. Levinson's theory of adult development (Levinson 1978).[14] Levinson breaks down adult life into four main eras: early, middle, late and late late adulthood. Early adulthood lasts from late adolescence through the mid-forties and it is "the most dramatic of all four eras". For men, mental and biological capacities are at their peak. Yet while struggling to "find his place in society" he must balance conflicting commitments to marriage, job, family and profession at a time when he is still burdened by the "residues of childhood conflicts".

Middle adulthood lasts from about 40 through to the mid-sixties. Around age 40, a man begins to experience changes in biological and psychological functioning. Usually, these changes are part of a subtle, gradual decline, but they may also be abrupt unexpected crises. At such time, a man is less driven by the instinctive energies of adolescence and early adulthood and, if successful, has achieved an increasingly "senior" place in his job and in society. In generational terms, he begins to leave youth and the initiation generation and joins the "Dominant Generation" (Gasset 1954). Wisdom, unsentimental compassion, breadth of vision and a "tragic sense of Life" (Unomuno) are positive qualities which may ripen in this season of a man's life. Intense, romantic impassioned creativity of the first half of life gives way to a more "sculpted" creativity (Jacques 1965).

Death takes on a new reality, not as something which happens to other people or by accident but as the "experience of one's own mortality" within one's life cycle. "Dealing with his mortality means that a man must engage in mourning for the dying self of youth, so that the self can be made more whole." (Levinson 1978:26).

Late adulthood, which lasts from around 60 through to the mid-eighties is characterized by "numerous biological, psychological and social changes". Serious disability, chronic illnesses, death of significant others, reduced reaction time, decreased inability to master new material, retirement and increasing frequency of death and loss are the challenges of this era. This transition marks a shift from the Dominant Generation to the Generation of Old Age.

Levinson describes poignantly the developmental tasks of the transition to "old age":

The developmental task is to overcome the splitting of youth and age, and find in each season an appropriate balance of the two. In late adulthood the archetypal figure of age dominates, but it can take various forms of the creative wise elder as long as a man retains his connection to youthful vitality, to the forces of growth in self and world. During the Late Adult Transition, man fears that the youth within him is dying and that only the old man - an empty, dry structure devoid of energy, interests or inner resources - will survive for a brief and foolish old age. (Levinson 1978:35).

Men need to be able to devote themselves in serious playfullness to "the voices within the self". But "to gain a genuine sense of integrity, a man must confront his lack of of integrity in his life" with times of "utter despair", that life has been of no value to himself and others. Worst of all, the damage is done: there is no further opportunity to right the balance. In contrast, the joys of this season are grandparenting, greater wisdom, perspective and "old age" style of creativity, plus "the role of a respected counselor-elder".

Since many people are living into their eighties and beyond, Levinson hypothesizes a further developmental era, Late Late Adulthood. The major aspects are a narrow or constriction of the life structure that it "contains only a small territory, a few significant relationships and a preoccupation with immediate bodily needs and personal comforts" (p. 38). Preparing for one's own death is a major developmental task: "To be able to involve himself in living he must make his peace with dying". Living may be devoid of meaning or receive new significance, life may appear meaningless or he may find ways to give it, life and death, his living and his dying, new significance, "reaching his ultimate involvement with the self".

The life structure, the basic pattern or design of a person's life at a given time, includes the individual's sociocultural world, his self, both conscious and unconscious, and his participation in the world i.e. how self and world are mutually interacting. The life structure is revealed through an individual's choices, important "marker events" and culminating points, showing self-in-the-world and world-in-the-self.

Levinson's main discovery was that life structure is age related and evolves through an orderly sequence during the adult years, as it does in pre-adult era. Moreover, each era is made up of a number of series of alternating stable and transitional periods. The stable period are those years in which a person invests and makes his choices in and pursue his goals and values within this life structure. In time, usually after 6-10 years, the life structure for internal and external reasons is disrupted, comes into question and must be modified. Such a phase is called a "transitional period" which serves to close the existing life structure and create the possibilites for a new one. Transitions may be mild or turbulent crises, but they are times of reassessment of the place and focus of self-and-world within the life structure. Transitions push one to ask "What have I done? Where am I now? Of what value is my life to society, to others, to myself?"

Transitions often last 4-5 years. The Early Adult Transition involves separating from life as an adolescent and child and making preliminary steps into an adult identity. This transition is followed by a stable period, "Entering the Adult World", in which his focus moves from his family of origin into a "novice adult" with a home base of his own, making initial choices regarding occupation, love relationships (usually including marriage and family), peer relationships, values, and life style. In Erikson's theory of the life cycle, this is the phase in which the dialectic between intimacy and isolation is paramount.

Around 30, at the Age Thirty Transition, a voice within the self says: "If I am to change my life - I must now make a start, for soon it will be too late." For most of Levinson's men, this transition was a severe crisis. These three periods - early adult transition, entering the adult world and age 30 - constitute the novice phase of early adulthood.

Settling Down is the stable period which follows and lasts most of the thirties. It is focused on establishing oneself and "making it", in moving up the ladder. In the late thirties especially, he may "Become His Own Man" (BOOM), and define a 'personal enterprise, a direction in which to strive, a sense of the future, a "project" as Sartre has termed it. The BOOM time terminates in the Mid-Life Transition, which raises once again all the more, the questioning: "What have I done with my life? What do I really get from and give my wife, children, friends, work, community - and self. What do I truly want for myself and others?" The stable period of Middle Adulthood is very much determined by the success or satisfaction of previous balancing needs of self and world. In Erikson's terms this is the time for "generativity versus stagnation", an enduring interest in and concern for the next and future generations or feeling stuck, static, not going anywhere. Levinson posits an Age Fifty Transition to Later Midde Adulthood analogous to Settling Down, and a further important transition to Late Adulthood, but he has less to say about these phases. To really understand the life cycle, one must be in a sense looking back at it, and so as we learn to look back without losing the ability to see ahead we shall know more about Late Adulthood and beyond.

Using Biblical ages as relative indicators of Abraham's life cycle by cutting years in half, we can say that Abram leaves Haran at the end of Settling Down period, breaking out of a stagnant life structure. Gen. 12-13 is part of his mid-life transition and Gen. 14-16 his entry in Middle Adulthood: Building a New Life Structure. The birth of Ishmael is the marker event of which ends the mid-life transition. The stable period of middle adulthood is passed over in silence by the text. Abraham, renamed, has a tumultous Age Fifty transition, including circumcision, name change, rejection of his first promised son and the promised birth of a second son, as well one last move.

The exile of Ishmael and Hagar is another marker event ending this period of transition. The childhood of Isaac is the focus of a second middle adulthood life structure, which includes much greater public recognition. A final crisis of generativity takes place during the transition from middle to late adulthood. Abraham has a particularly active and creative late adulthood, fathering more children, arranging for continuity of the next generation, but also burying his wife and preparing for his own death during his late late adulthood.

Biblical Biography

The main narrative section of the Bible, Genesis through Kings, is told mostly through the lives of the main protagonists.[15] Exodus is very much the lifestory of Moses; the rise of the monarchy, the intertwined lives of Samuel, Saul and David. Except perhaps for David and Jacob, no life history is given in full. The story of Isaac is fragmentary; even the more detailed account of Joseph (and to an extent Jacob) focuses on his early and mid-adult period.

Biblical biography is not concerned with a person's cognitive or psychosexual development but rather his unfolding destiny. As such, early childhood, felt to be so crucial in contemporary psychobiography and psychoanalysis, is usually ignored in Biblical context. Instead, antenatal events, circumstances concerning conception and birth which might indicate **destiny**, are given prominence. In Genesis, naming is an important part of receiving one's destiny. But above all, the birth of a son is **the** major life event.

The most common and concise "Biblical biography" is as part of a geneological list. Such a biography presents a person in his main social role, as that of a paternal ancestor, part of an unfolding chain of sons becoming fathers. It is the birth of a son, in patriarchal culture, which **is** the most important marker event in one's life since this guarantees that one will become an ancestor and not "cut off". Hence the age at the birth of a son is the major marker event in a person's life cycle separating everything which came before from all which is to follow. Having a son assures one of what men most desire, a sense of "symbolic immortality" a feeling of ongoing continuity (Lifton 1970; 1979).

The sense of continuity is reinforced by knowing where a person is buried. In the time of Kings, for example, almost always the burial site of the monarch is mentioned. In Genesis, almost all the main actors are buried together and it is Joseph's dying wish to buried as an ancestor in his ancestral land. Such a gathering of bones create a community of dead ancestors "which are at once a focus of unity and community for the living, as well as a guiding presence, a lasting symbol of the groups' continuity" (Bloch 1971).

Abraham's life history focused only on the akeda is often called a "story of faith and obedience" but seen within the life cycle perspective, it becomes a search for continuities. To elaborate this point, allow me a diversion into the nature of inheritance and succession.

Succession: Geneological or Charismatic?

Continuity or succession usually follows one of two patterns: a) geneological, or inheritance by birthright and b) charismatic, or inheritance by selection and ability, i.e. by being "chosen". The benefits of the geneological pattern is assured transition. Everybody knows who will be the next leader, king or priest. The dangers are that the new leader may be unfit for the job. The charismatic pattern involves the complementary benefits and dangers. One receives a man capable and right for the office, but may involve a period of uncertainty, even civil war, until the succession is assured.[16]

The period of the Judges is a time of charismatic leadership in which local leaders arose in times of crisis, but no reliable mechanism existed to provide for institutionalized leadership and succession. Samuel, a charismatic leader, against his better judgement introduced geneological succession and institution of hereditary kingship. Independent prophets still arose, like Elijah, Isaiah, Amos and Jeremiah, who provided a charismatic type of moral leadership which could influence but not replace hereditary rule. The Book of Kings is full of stories of bad hereditary rulers.

Moses was a charismatic leader par excellence. He left political leadership, charismatic, appointing his successor Joshua in place of his own sons. Instead he created a priestly and levite class which would be inherited from father to son. His compromise, therefore was to mold a charismatic political leadership with a hereditary priest caste.

Abraham lived in a clan context in which the head of the clan was "both and together" religious and political chief. He did have dilemmas within his family concerning who would be his geneoloical heir and whether it was up to him to decide. He also wished that his son would inherit his charismatic function, with its special relation to his God. To put it another way, Abraham wanted his son not only to be head of the clan, "pater familias" but also priest and prophet, i.e. to combine geneological succession with the charismatic.

Failures of the Fathers

The tension between hereditary and charismatic succession is brought into sharp relief when one reviews the relations between fathers and sons in the main narrative texts of Genesis-First Kings. Bluntly stated, there are few if any good fathers and few, if any, instances of uncomplicated hereditary succession. Within Genesis, neither Adam, Noah, Isaac, Jacob, Reuben, Judah or even Joseph can be described as successful fathers. In the later Books, Moses, Aaron, Gideon, Avimelech, Eli, Samuel, Saul, David and even Solomon are failures in most aspects in their fathering abilities (cf. Table 1: Fathers and Sons). Most undergo severe traumatic loss in relation to their sons and except for the hereditary desent of the priesthood and later kingship, there is no clear-cut case where a father successfully initiates his first born son to be his chosen spiritual successor.

Perhaps the most touching and tender moment between a son and his father concerns just such a missed opportunity for hereditary and spiritual continuity when Isaac and Esau, together learn to their horror about Jacob's trick:

> *No sooner had Jacob left the presence of his father Issac - after Isaac had finished blessing Jacob - than his brother Esau came back from the hunt. He too prepared a tasty dish and brought it to his father. And he said to his father, "Let my father sit up and eat of his son's game, so that you may give me your innermost blessing." His father Issac said to him, "Who are you?" And he said, "I am your son, Esau, your first born!" Isaac was seized with very violent trembling "Who was it then," he demanded "that hunted game and brought it to me? Moreover, I ate of it before you came, and I blessed him; now he must remain blessed!" When Esau heard his father's words, he burst into wild and bitter sobbing and said to his father, Bless me too Father!... Have you but one blessing, Father? Bless me too, Father!". And Esau wept aloud* (27:30-40).

From this paternal perspective, it is considerably easier to make sons than to pass onto them a special relation to the Divine, which is the Biblical hallmark of charismatic leadership.

In the context of the failures of the fathers, Abraham's conscious decision to offer up his son is all the more remarkable.

Table 1:
Fathers and Sons in the Bible

Father	Son	Comment
Adam	Cain, Abel	(Genesis 4:8-16) Father loses both sons in one blow: one to death, the other to exile (cf. David)
Adam	Seth	"Replacement" child, without whom father would be "cut off". (Genesis 4:25)
Noah	Ham	Father sexually exposed by son; curses his son's son in revenge (9:21-27)
Terah	Haran	Dies in lifetime of father (11:28)
Terah	Abram	Son abandons father in late adulthood (11:32-12:4)
Terah	Nahor	No information available (cf. 11:31 in which Nahor is missing)
Abraham	Ishmael	Father ostracizes son (21:9-14)
Abraham	Issac	Father almost kills son as part of ritual sacrifice (22:1-19)
Isaac	Jacob	Father tricked into given blessing to "wrong" son (27:1-29)
Isaac	Esau	Tragic mismeeting when blessing stolen; perhaps the most tender moment of a son and father in Genesis (27:30-40)

Fathers and Sons in the Bible (cont'd)

Jacob	Reuven	Son sexually betrays father (35:22); offers for father to kill son's son as surety for Benjamin (42:37)
Jacob	Judah	responds to paternal favoritism by hatching plot against Joseph, misleads father about Joseph's fate (37:26-8)
Jacob	Joseph	parental preference leads to murderous sibling jealousy; father mourns interminably (37:3-4; 37:32-35); emotionally unavailable to surviving sons.
Jacob	Benjamin	Father overprotective as part of interminable mourning syndrome (44:20-34)
Joseph	Ephraim, Menashe	Unable to get his father to bless first born (48:1-20)
Judah	Er, Onan	Father loses two sons; overprotective of youngest son. Replacement twins born (38:1-30)
Moses	Gershon	Father fails to circumcize first born son, who is almost killed returning to Egypt; son plays no public role (Exodus 4:24-6)
Eli	Hafni, Pinchas	Corrupt sons die in battle when Holy Ark captured (I Sam 4:11)
Samuel	Yoel, Aviya	Corrupt sons, not worthy to succeed father (I Sam 8:1-22)

Fathers and Sons in the Bible (cont'd)

Saul	Jonathan	Father condemns son to death (I Sam 14:24-45); Father feels betrayed by son (I Sam 20:30-31); Father and son die in battle (I Sam 31:6)
David	Amnon, Abshalom	Father loses both sons in one blow - one to death, the other to exile (cf. Adam); Abshalom later returns, rebels and is killed. Father cries "Would that I had died in your place" (II Sam 19)
David	Adonijah	Son rebels against aging father (I Kings 1:5-6)
David	Solomon	Son is crowned in a palace coup against aging impotent king (I Kings 1:7-39)
Solomon	Rehavam	Phallic rivalry between son and father (I Kings 12:10)

Fathers and mothers	Rebellious son who does not listen to parents	Parents take son and denounce him to elders at city gate, where he will be executed by public stoning. (Deuteronomy 21:18)

CHAPTER THREE:
LIFE WITH FATHER

Once God is dead and the commandment to Honor Thy Father is denigrated, there are no limits to narcissism, and there is no way home to the continuity of generations or the community of persons.
- Stephen A. Shapiro, Manhood: A New Definition

Is my God, the God of my Father?

We inherit religion, the God of Father (and Mother) along with the rest of our cultural baggage. At some point we must take a stance vis à vis this God of our Father. If we merely go along with it, without developing our own authentic relation to God of the Father, then religious tradition becomes merely conventional, without an inner relation to these ultimate concerns. Age-graded rituals and initiations seek to instill in the young devotee a relation which is at once personal, authentic and yet at the same time essentially a continuity of the tradition of the fathers and mothers. Alternatively one can reject the God of one's parents. This rejection can be twofold. I can reject their religion in inner or external forms, or I can affirm another competing tradition, such is the difference between atheists, seekers and converts.

The tension between continuity and disruption, between obedience and revelation, between paternalistic authority and filial self-exploration is a drama acted out in every generation, but it is particularly acute in times of radical change.

There are a few hints at the sources of Abram's disenchantment with the religion of his father - the death of his brother, his own childlessness, and early migration all in their way threaten continuity and conventional pathways of symbolic immortality. Loyalty to the God of the Father, would still leave him "cut off."

Yonina Talmon, in her study of "Family and Community in Kibbutz," has shown that for an innovative, revolutionary society, the ties of family clash with the bonds of "revolutionary fellowship"[17]:

Kinship is based on maintenance of intergenerational ties and a certain basic continuity of transmitted tradition. Rejection of this continuity lead to a revolt against the authority of the older generation and disrupts cross-generational ties. Kinship is essentially non-selective and non-ideological. Members of a

revolutionary elite substitute for the ascriptive natural ties a
Wahlverwandschaft *, an elective kinship, based on spontaneous communion*
of kindred souls and an identification with a common mission. Ideology
becomes the dominant unifying factor. Although solidarity among comrades
is very intense and is a highly significant integrating factor, it must be viewed
in context: it is firmly embedded in the commitment to the revolutionary cause
and is subsumed in it. Fellowship is rooted in a common idea and a common
will. Relatives and friends who do not share this commitment become outsiders,
almost strangers... (Talmon 1972:3).

Other spiritual revolutionaries opt for a non-kin based solidarity of the faithful,
"an elective kinship, based on spontaneous communion of kindred souls and on an
identification with a common mission" (Talmon 1972:3). Jesus, as revealed in the
Gospel of Matthew, is one such innovator who explicitly rejects family as a basis
for his spiritual revolution. When members of his family come to visit him, he
replies:

"Who is my mother? Who are my brothers?" And stretching out his hand
toward his disciples he said, "Here are my mother and my brothers. Anyone
who does the will of my Father in heaven; he is my brother and sister and
mother.

(Matthew 12:46-50).

In other more harsh phrases he speaks of overt conflict within the family:
"Brother will betray brother and father his children, children will rise against their
parents"; or even more passionately:

Do not suppose that I have come to bring peace to earth, it is not peace, I have
come to bring a sword. For I have come to set a man against his father a
daughter against his mother, a daughter-in-law against her mother-in-law. A
man's enemies will be those of his own household

(Mat. 10:34-6)

Yonina Talmon (1972:3f) hypothesized that in the revolutionary phase of collective
movement, "there is a certain fundamental incompatibility between commitment to a
radical revolutionary ideology and intensive collective identification on the one hand,
and family solidarity on the other". Although Talmon was examining the earlier
revolutionary phase of the kibbutz, many of her conclusions apply to any revolutionary

innovation, the clash between the new and old, between ideology and family.
Such is the dilemma of every revolutionary founder. After having broken with
the past to create a new order, how does the revolutionary protect the innovation
without itself succumbing to a new revolutionary break? Or in other terms, how
does one assure that the children of the revolution remain loyal to the ideals of the
new order – without breaking from this new order. i.e. how to be loyal to a
"tradition of disloyalty". The dilemma can be seen in Communist Russia, China,
Israeli kibbutz etc. It is not surprising for revolutionary founders to hold onto
power for so long that they emasculate the successor generation. Or to return to
Abraham who might say, "How can I trust my son not to abandon his father, as I
abandoned my father?"

The Biblical text is sensitive to this issue of continuity and abandonment. A
casual reading of the transition between Chapters 11-12 give one a sense that
Abraham's father Terah died at Haran and subsequently Abraham received his
decisive call, "Leave your country, your family, your father's house..." (12:1). But
an examination of the dates of Abram's departure and his father's death reveal that
Abram did not leave Kharan* after his father died. Abram was 75 when he left
Kharan and was born when his father was approximately 70. As a result Terah, his
father was about 145 Biblical Years Old at the time of his son's departure. Since the
last verse of ch. 11 states that Terah was 205 when he died he was very much alive
when Abram abandoned Kharan, indeed he had about 60 Biblical years left to live.

Closer examination of the geneological formulae serve to emphasize the point.
In the first list of descendants from Adam to Noah the geneologic formula is as
follows: age at birth of first son, number of years lived after birth of son, as well as
fathering other sons and daughters and a final statement of total lifespan. For
example:

*When Jared was a hundred and sixty-two years old he became the father of
Enoch. After the birth of Enoch, Jared lived for eight hundred years and he
became the father of sons and daughters. In all, Jared lived for nine hundred
and sixty-two years; and then he died.*

(5:18-20)

---

*   Note: English translations often render Abram's brother הרן and the city where Terah moved to
and died in, חרן both as "Haran". In the Hebrew, they are distinct. Unless quoting a Biblical
passage in translation I have tried to differentiate the two by referring to Terah's son as
"Haran" and the city as "Kharan", in keeping with the phonology of the Hebrew text.

In the second list of descendants descibed after the flood, from Noah to Terah, the statement of total lifespan is ommitted e.g. "When Eber was thirty-four years old he became father of Peleg. After the birth of Peleg, Eber lived four hundred and thirty years and became the father of sons and daughters." (11:16-17). The case of Terah is once again anomalous. As we have seen, the age at the birth of his sons is given, "When Terah was seventy years old he became the father of Abram, Nahor and Haran" (11:26) and a few lines later the statement of total lifespan is given, "Terah's life lasted two hundred and five years and he died in Haran." (11:32).

What is conspicuously left out is the number of years (145) he lived after the birth of his sons. And why? Because it would appear too obvious that Abram did not follow the commandment of "honor thy mother and father" but did in fact leave a living father behind in Kharan. The fact that the text is subtly reworked to disguise this reveals how sensitive an issue of parental abandonment remained.[18]

Life With Father

From Abraham's "life with father" we know only a few facts. He was born when his father was old, probably a laterborn second son; he and his father were born in the southern end of Mesopotamia and dreamed of going to the other end of the Fertile Crescent but stopped half way in the northern hills of Mesopotamia in southern Kurdistan, today near the Turkish-Syrian border. He married Sarai, whose name, although not explained by the text means, "princess". So it is possible but by no means certain that she was of noble birth or somehow connected with Mesopotamian cult (Teubel 1984). What is peculiar is that her geneology is not given, while that of her sister-in-law, Milcah is (11:29).[19] Milcah is "the daughter of Haran, the father of Milcah and Iscah" This "Haran" is presumably the same as Haran the brother of Abram[20] - in which case Milcah is her husband's niece, a pattern of parallel cousin marriage still common in Kurdistan (Barth 1954).

Rashi, the great medieval Hebrew Biblical commentator identifies "Iscah" as "Sarai", as though Abram also practiced father's brother's daughter marriage - the two brothers, marrying two sisters, their nieces. Sarai as Abram's paternal niece would fit with what Abraham says to the king of Gerar: "She is in truth my sister, my father's daughter though not my mother's and she became my wife" - here "sister" and father's "daughter" are used in a classificatory or metaphorical sense of close female relative, as in cultures in which a niece would be literally called "sister".

However, if Iscah is Sarai, why does the text not clearly say so? And if Sarai is not Iscah, who is she? Since her origins seem to be left mysterious - deliberately deleted like Cain's words to Abel - to obscure her past and allow her to appear on the Biblical stage "Ex nihilo" - independent of any "past".

What we do know definitely about her at this stage is that Sarai was "barren, she had no child" (11:30). The phrase "barren,...no child" may be a hendiadys (two words to indicate one concept like "hue and cry" in English) (Alter 1985:72). But I suspect the text is saying more. The Hebrew, עקרה אין לה ולד "akara ein la valad" uses both a common term for infertility, "akara" from the verbal root "akar", to be uprooted, and an unusual term "valad" which appears only here in all Scripture. In modern Hebrew "valad" can mean "fetus" or "embryo" as well as "child" (Alcalay 1970) and that is the intention here, I believe. The text is suggesting that the cause of Sarai's barreness is not miscarriage or stillborns, but primary infertility, the inability to conceive.

In the development of spiritual breakthroughs, the innovator is often set on his path by some personal tragedy or traumatic life event: infertility in the case of

Abram, an existential awareness of suffering and death for Siddartha Buddha; death of a brother to Ataturk etc. Somehow the innovator is able to use this personal crisis – "a crucial period of increased vulnerability and heightened potential" (Erikson 1963:12) - to grapple with universal human dilemmas.

Genesis vs. Oedipus

In Mesopotamian culture, fertility was regarded as proof of spiritual virility and directly linked to a man's self-esteem (Pritchard 1969; Cassuto 1964; Jacobsen 1967; Orlinsky 1964). Not to have sons was considered a major life tragedy. The lack of sons also posed economic hardship in such a labor-intensive pastoral economy. According to some ancient legal documents, (De Vaux 1978; Speiser 196; Sarna 1966) a woman who did not produce children was subject to divorce or other extraordinary treatment. Abram probably did not or could not divorce his wife because of their double bond of kinship, as wife and paternal "sister". Edward Said, in his study of "Beginnings" has suggested that "what overwhelmed Oedipus is the burden of plural identities incapable of coexisting within one person" (Said 1975:170). In a culture in which a man might marry his "sister" Abram does not seem overwhelmed by his "plural identities" and perhaps that helps explain the relative absence of Oedipal conflict in Genesis.

The story of Oedipus begins as a tale of child abuse. The Theban King, Laius (together with his Queen Joscasta) desires to kill his newborn son because an oracle had warned that this child would be his father's murderer. The infant is left to die but, by chance, saved by an old sheperd couple who raise the child as their own.

Oedipus subsequently does unknowingly kill his father and by resolving the mystery of the Sphinx ("What walks on four in the morning, two in the afternoon and three in the evening?) saves his native city and unknowingly marries his mother, Jocasta. Freud, systematically misread the beginning of the myth by ignoring the "filicidal urge" on the part of Oedipus' parents (Besançon 1974). Recent revisions of psychoanalytic theory (Ross; Shapiro; Samuels; Osterow) emphasize the destructive impact of lack of fathering and suggest that Oedipal neurosis occurs only when parents play out destructive or seductive parental roles toward their children, i.e. act as Oedipal parents, along the lines of Laius and Jocasta.

Part of Freud's misreading of Oedipus is the result of his focus on a "child-centered psychology". Indeed, much of psychoanalytic thought is presented from the son's point of view exclusively. In contrast, Biblical psychology, especially Genesis, is "father centered". The akeda is presented from the father's perspective not the son's. The Biblical equivalent of Laius is Pharaoh (Exodus 1:16-22) in Old Testament (and King Herod in the New Testament) as if to suggest that the filicidal urge to get rid of son-competitors is a basic aspect of power complex within the paternal psyche. It is as if when power issues dominate, even an Abraham may become a pharaoh.

Aside from the akeda, however, the main conflicts in Genesis are not between parent and child (intergenerational conflict) but rather between siblings (intragenerational conflict). From Cain and Abel, Noah's sons Shem and Ham to Isaac and Ishmael, Jacob and Esau, Joseph and his brothers, Reuben and Judah, Judah's sons Er and Onan - the main conflict is between brothers. Such a brotherly rivalry, we have argued, provides the unifying frame of the Book of Genesis (resolved only with the coming together of another set of brothers, Moses and Aaron), and again suggests that sibling rivalry is a fundamental fact of family life, a fact reflected in rivalries over reproductive envy among wives (Hagar and Sarah), or sister-wives (Leah and Rachel). Jealousy reaches murderous proportions when fueled by parental favoritism - whether by God, in the case of Cain and Abel, or by Jacob in the case of Joseph and his brothers.*

Two more texts focus on sexual tensions between fathers and daughters (or daughters-in-law). Lot and Judah, in chapters 19 and 38, both unconsciously have sexual relations with "daughters", presumably reflecting the unconscious sexual desire of fathers toward their female offspring.

The realities of the Biblical psyche for the father, therefore, include filicidal urges, favoritism between chosen and unchosen children, illicit sexual wishes toward daughters, all of which unless checked may have disasterous effects. For the psychology of the Biblical Mother, delayed fertility provokes bitter reproductive envy and ultimately overidentification with the promised child; once again maternal, like paternal favoritism, encourages fratricidal conflict. In the Biblical life history, however, there is a countervailing force of initiation into one's divinely inspired destiny, the need for self creation, even self-naming which transcends the family cycle.

The family dynamics of the four generations which comprise the Patriarchal Narratives (Genesis 12-50) set off the universal issues of power and envy with one's personal father against the possibilty of individuation and a personal destiny under guidance of a spiritual father.

---

*   Don W. Forsyth's interesting article "Sibling Rivalry, Aesthetic Sensibility and Social Structure in Genesis", Forsyth (1991) develops many of these themes but appeared too late to be discussed in the text.

"The effect of sibling death is probably greatly underestimated ...After the death of a child, parents are likely to be anxious about their next child, and this may take the form of being overprotective. "It is not unusual for parents to find themselves watching their sleeping child and envisioning how they are going to react if they should find this child dead, too"

Kalish 1985:237.

Sibling Survivor

If childlessness is one great issue for Abram, then the other must be the unexpected death of his brother, Haran. Here again the Hebrew text suggests the disruptive impact of this loss: "Haran died in the lifetime of his father Terah, in his native land" (11:28).

The Hebrew על־פני "al pnei", here translated as "the lifetime" literally means "before the face", "on the face" in the sense of "in front of" as in other translations: "Haran died in the presence of his father Terah" (J.B.); "And Haran died before his father Terah" (K.J.). The death of a son in the lifetime of a father suggests the most fundamental disruption of the "ancestral order" of sons following fathers. The death of a son, and in this case probably his firstborn, is as great a threat to biological continuity (Lifton 1970) as infertility. Abram would have experienced both threats to continuity. The death of a son would have been all the more traumatic since Terah had long awaited the birth of a child.

The loss of a sibling would have had repercussions for Abraham. The death of someone close to him made the reality of physical extinction agonizingly poignant. It is further likely that his continued survival, when his brother did not, induced a sense of ambivalent "survivor guilt".[21] On the one hand, by Haran's death, Abram probably acceded to the role of "first" son, even a "replacement child", and major heir, heightening his sense of being special and specially chosen (Erikson 1963). On the other hand, such a rise in status was achieved at the cost of his brother's life. Abram, moreover, would face the survivor's question: "Why do I continue to live when my brother died?"

The Loss of Both Brothers?

A close reading of the description of the death of Haran ("Haran died in the lifetime of his father Terah, in his native land, Ur of the Chaldeans"[22] 11:28), reveals an ambiguity. Does "this native land" refer to Terah, the father or Haran, the son? Most commentators read "his" as Terah's and assume that the entire clan was native to Ur, one of the great cities of the ancient world, "the cradle of Sumarian civilization" (cf. Kramer 1950; Hallo & Simpson 1963; Wooley 1935; Pritchard 1969). The difficulty with this reading lies in the use of the Hebrew word "moledet", מולדת here translated as "native land".

In the next chapter, the call to Abram (12:1-5) "Go forth from your country, your native land, your father's house" uses "moledet". There, "moledet" probably also denotes "native land" but has also been translated as "kindred" (K.J.) or "family" (JB). The difficulty with the latter interpretations lies in differentiating kindred or family from the last term in the triad. Abram must leave, i.e. "his father's house", which also seems to indicate kinship bonds he must sever. If Abraham's native land is Ur, then 'his country' may refer to Haran, suggesting Abram must **not** return to the land of his birth.

An intriguing view, suggested by Ramban, sees "his" as contrastive, that is, reading the verse "Haran died in **his** native land"; his and not theirs. It is possible that Haran alone was native to Ur while the rest of the clan derived from elsewhere, allowing "moledet" of 12:1 to refer to the city Haran as Abram's place of birth.

The tragedy of losing a child, whether in one's native land or worse, in exile, might provide Terah with the motive for the major dislocation - to move away to make a new start by removing himself physically, and so psychologically, from the scene of the loss.

The final event in the "Life with Father" novice phase of adulthood is the family migration from Ur. The Text states, "Terah took his son, Abram..." The Hebrew verb ויקח "va-yikakh" is a verb of power, indicting that Terah was firmly in charge of his patriarchal extended family. Each individual who accompanied Terah is referred to both by name and by social standing:

his son Abram, his grandson Lot, the son of Haran, and his daughter-in-law Sarai, the wife of his son Abram.

Most noteably, Sarai is given a double status as daughter-in-law and wife to his son, with the relationship to the Father given precedence over her relation to her husband, Abram. Within the entourage, it seems, social status exists patriarchally, in relation to Father.

Missing also in the account of this first trek is Abram's younger brother Nahor. It appears that Nahor was seperated from the clan at this time, and that Abram in a life-historical sense, lost both his brothers. Cut off from counterbalancing support of his brothers, Abram would become all the more dependent upon his father (and his father upon him). Such an overemphasis of the importance of Father is reflected in the meaning of Abram's name (discussed in detail below).

There is no life history of Nahor, beyond his "generative" role as a progenitor and ancestor, and his absence is a precursor of shadowy relationships between subsequently chosen and unchosen brothers: Issac - Ishmael; Jacob - Esau; Joseph and his brothers.

Remarkably, Nahor's name and geneology appear immediately after the story of the akeda, when Abraham learns that "Milcah too has borne children to your brother Nahor", (22:20-24) along with the rest of his descendants, including his future daughter-in-law Rebekah. A further note in the marriage negotiations (Ch. 24) indicates that a northern Mesopotamian town, Aram-Haharaim, is "the city of Nahor" (24:10) suggesting that he, too, ended up in the Haran region. What, then, is the link between the absence of Nahor, Terah's move and the akeda? I take a clue from a word motif which begins at this point and reverberates, in the language of the akeda itself, the Hebrew word for "together", "yakhdav" יחדו. When Terah takes his troop, it is said, "and they set out together" (11:31); when Abram takes his entourage it is written, "and they said set out" - no together is added. The same contrastive verbal play is played out in akeda. What is the meaning of such contrasting "togetherness - separateness": a formal togetherness of the patriarchal family or an authentic coming together of the spirit? Terah, as Father, took his family together; the irony, the lack of a spiritual union, is only apparent on rereading. Abram set out, but was not "together". He was involved in searching for a new kind of "togetherness". In mid-life, the issues of "being together", or being cut off from one self and across the generations, are central issues for all those who aspire to be a generative man.

To sum up the text "Terah took his son Abram, his grandson Lot the son of Haran, and his daughter-in-law Sarai, the wife of his son Abram and they set out together..." (11:31) stresses two points. First, Terah "took" Abram, clearly showing that Terah was firmly in charge of the family unit. Second, each individual who accompanied Terah is referred by name and by social standing, in the case of Sarah by her double status, daughter-in-law and wife. Finally, the record does not indicate that Abram's surviving brother, Nahor, accompanied them on the journey. Much later (24:10) another city "Aram-naharaim", i.e. Aram of the two rivers i.e. of Mesopotamia (?) is mentioned as "the city of Nahor". Ramban (Nachmonides), another great medieval commentator, argues that only Haran was born in Ur and the rest of the family derived from the Haran area, the stay in the south being only a temporary sojourn. This interpretation allows one to interpret "moledet" in the call from Haran (12:1) as "native land". But if Nahor did not accompany Terah and his entourage, was it because, with children, unlike Abram, he was already independent of his father?

"Breaking Out"

In Levinson's terminology, staying with father means that a son can never "become one's own man". The mid-life transition thus becomes a developmental crisis of which Levinson describes five possible sequences: Advancement within a stable life structure (which for Abraham would mean continuing to stay on within his father's domain); serious failure or decline within a stable life structure or even a chaotic structure. But Abram's response seems to correspond most closely to Sequence C: "Breaking Out: Trying for a New Life Structure".

According to Levinson, Breaking Out often includes a distinctive marker event, such as leaving a wife, quitting a job, or moving to another region. For the next few years a man makes a concerted effort to build a new structure more in accord with his own values and aspirations. Unfortunately, it is extremely difficult to make a radical change at this time of life. The new structure is likely to be a compromise. By 40, he may have made important changes in his situation, but he is still involved in relationships he had seemingly given up when he took the decisive step, and is not able to devote himself sufficiently to his new activities and choices. (Levinson 1977:206).

Breaking out does seem to fit the pattern of activities of Abraham in the initial years of wandering from Mesopotamia to Canaan, on to Egypt, back to Canaan at least until the "brit ben habitarim", the covenant between the pieces (15:6f). At that time, Abram reborn as Abraham, is able to resolve young/old polarity and has come face to face with destruction/creation polarity, which are main tasks of mid-life individuation. With the birth of one son and then another and finally many others, he is able to resolve his yearning for a biological mode of symbolic immortality. A final polarity which Levinson discusses - "attachment/separateness" - is only to be resolved at the akeda and after.

Another notion which Levinson discusses is the shift from being "junior" to being more "senior": "to combine authority and mutuality - accepting his own responsibility and offering leadership, yet also inviting their (junior's) participation and fostering their growth toward greater independence and authority" (op,cit. p.29-30). Within his "father's house" and culture, Abraham must remain in "junior" status so long as he is without children; likewise a woman's position would normally remain insecure, so long as she could not produce an heir for her husband's family. On the other hand there is a hint in Gen 12:5. When Abram leaves his father's house he takes, besides his wife and nephew, "all the wealth that they had amassed, and the persons that they had acquired in Haran". No one is sure who these "persons" are[23] - whether religious converts, members of his household, slaves or whatever. It does show that Abram was not without successful leadership qualities.

The call to leave one's country, native land and father's house or kindred is a call not only to depart from an uncreative past but for an undefined promised and promising future. The leaving is as much "leaving **From**" as a "going **To**". When he set out from his father's house in Kharan he did not know his destination, like a man in mid-life crisis setting out on a unknown outward and inner journey. That the destination turned out to be the land of Canaan allows us to make a number of inferences concerning his initial relation to God and father.

The language of Abram's passage from Kharan exactly parallels that of his father's from Ur:

> *Abram took his wife Sarai and his brother's son Lot...and all the wealth that they had amassed, and the persons that they had acquired in Haran, and they set out...*

(12:5).

The parallel suggests that Abram is clearly in charge of the entourage, as Terah had been before him. To the extent of in-camp authority, he has inherited his father's position. But the text subtly hints at the process of attaining the status of camp leader. In the passage before, the text reads, "Abram went forth as the Lord commanded him, and Lot went with him." The subtle change in the repeated information - that Lot accompanied him - is another case of semantic modification. When the idea to set out first occurred, Lot on his own decided to join, Abram did not "take" him. But once they got under way, he recognized Abram as the leader of the expedition and hence the phrase, "Abram took...Lot", his status within the list and presumably the camp behind Abram's wife Sarai. The repetition of the phrase "brother's son" shows that Abram relates to Lot via kinship roles, perhaps adopting him as an expression of survivor guilt toward his dead brother. When the two men return to Canaan after Egypt, however, there is no kinship epithet. He is referred to as Lot, a man in his own right and able to cope on his own. Later, when Abram sets out to rescue him, the narrative calls him first "son of Abram's brother" (14:12), but when the fugitive brings word to Abram and his allies, his he is referred to as אחיו "akhiv", literally "his brother"[24], perhaps like Sarai was called "sister", a classificatory sibling as when one may say "She is a 'sister' to me", or in cultures when all paternal nieces (Father's, Sister's, Daughters) are also called "sister".

One of the very few facts known about Abram's father is his original desire to travel to Canaan when he set out from Ur. For some unspecified reason he remained half way round the fertile crescent in Haran. Abram "unconsciously" completed his father's unfulfilled desire as if to say, "I have arrived, father, where you wanted to take us!".

His relation to the land of Canaan, however, is not connected with his own father but with a new spiritual Father. Thus Abram's first act in the development of his relation with his God was the fulfillment of his father's goal. One may infer that at this initial stage of his religious development, his relation to the Divine was modeled after his relation with his biological father.

Freud in a famous passage in the Interpretation of Dreams, writes: "When we look back at this unashamed period of childhood it seems to us a Paradise; and Paradise itself is no more than a group fantasy of the childhood of the individual. That is why mankind was naked in Paradise and without shame in one another's presence; until a moment arrived when shame and anxiety awoke, expulsion followed and sexual life and the tasks of cultural activity began. But we can regain this Paradise every night in our dreams" (Freud 1975:343).

Freud, like Marx, felt that religion was a collective neurosis, an "illusion" which mankind needed to outgrow like other childish anxieties. While it does seem true that religious feeling and conceptions of the Divine do have their roots in childhood feelings toward all powerful parental figures, the Mother and Father archetype, an individual who maintains such a childish view of God into adulthood may be as fixated in his spiritual development as the neurotic in his psychosexual development.

Unlike theologians, psychologists can say nothing about God - He (and She) is beyond our province. Following Jung, what psychologists can legitimately study is a person's conception of God at various phases of his lifecycle. Jung called this "conception of the God", a person's "God-image", how God feels and seems to a person. We are not concerned with the validity of these God-images but rather how they develop within the unfolding of the personality. A Rabbinic maxim shows understanding of this issue when it states that in the Bible, God is revealed in the language of men i.e. in a way, they might know Him.

God of Abraham

The question concerning the nature of the God of Abraham has intrigued scholars and is revived anew with the discovery of new artifacts and texts. (De Vaux 1978; Mazar and references ad. loc.) There does seem to be a consensus that the "God of Abram" does fuse two very different conceptions of divinity in the ancient Near East. The first were household gods of Mesopotamia, "ila", who were guardians of family and household. These were usually small statues, possibly akin to "teraphim", which were at once portable and personal, familial-tribal divinities.

De Vaux 1978:272 states:

The god of the father was not tied to any sanctuary - he was above all connected with a group of men. He had revealed himself to the ancestor of these men and had been recognized by that ancestor. This link, which extended from the ancestor to the group descended from him, was regarded as a kind of kinship...The god of the father, then, was really a nomadic deity, leading, accompanying and guarding the group that was faithful to him, deciding where the people should go and keeping them safe on their way...In other words, the god of the father was deeply involved in the history of the group and guided it.

This god, who had revealed himself to the ancestors of the people and who remained "with him", was committed to those who were faithful to him by virtue of his promises...the promise of posterity, the promise of land or the promise of both posterity and land at the same time...These promises are completely in accordance with two fundamental desires experienced by semi-nomadic herdsman - the desire for posterity which will ensure continuity in the clan and the desire for land where they hope to settle.

The other divinity was the so-called "High God", who resided in fixed Temples at the symbolic center of each Mesopotamian Polis. Each city often had one Patron God, with elaborate cult and ritual, residential priests and priestess, "hieros gamos" - a celebration of ritual sacred marriage as a symbol of fertility. Based on a privileged position of the priests, it was a hierarchical, urban, ritualistic cult.

What was lacking in this Mesopotamian worldview was a conception of a universal moral order (Speiser 1964; Sarna 1966). In the Mesopotamian creation story **Enuma Elish** (Pritchard 1969), man is not created to fulfill some divine plan but to serve the gods, "that their life would be easy". Like the great rivers of

Mesopotamia, the gods could be whimsical, inconsistent. In contrast, the Egyptian societies, which grew up along the reliable Nile did develop an ethically consistent universe, a conception to which Abraham was exposed during his sojourn there. Moreover, wanderers, semi-nomads like the patriarchs on the move, require a God who is portable, a god available anywhere and everywhere.

To summarize Abram's Mesopotamian heritage: His God fuses a personal, tribal God, Protector of household and family, with a Creator High God (El Elyon), Creator of Heaven and Earth, who though vengeful, is bound by covenants and a universal moral order. From a psychological standpoint, Abram's God-image was on the one hand different from the god of his father, Terah, and on the other hand, based on an unconscious identification with his father's wishes or "father-ideal".

CHAPTER FOUR:
ABRAM AS WANDERER

The Call and the "Novice Phase"

According to Levinson, there are four developmental tasks of the novice phase, the first half of early adulthood. The first task is "forming a Dream and giving it a place in the life structure" (Levinson 1978:90).
According to Levinson, the Dream

> is a vague sense of self-in-adult-world. It has the quality of a vision, an imagined possibility that generates excitement and vitality. At the start it is poorly articulated and only tenuously connected to reality, although it may contain concrete image such as winning the Nobel Prize or making the all-star team. It may take a dramatic form as in the myth of the hero: the great artist, business tycoon, athletic or intellectual superstar performing magnificent feats and receiving special honors. It may take mundane forms...

> Whatever the nature of his Dream, a young man has the developmental task of giving it greater definition and finding ways to live it out. It makes a great difference in his growth whether his initial life structure is consonant with and infused by the Dream, or opposed to it...

The call from Kharan to "break out" from his father-bound life structure, was a concrete formulation of Abraham's Dream. The Dream provided a solution to the other developmental tasks of the "novice phase" which remained incomplete: forming mentor relationships, an occupation and love relationships, marriage and family. Of these tasks, the only one in which he had some success concerned occupation, earning a livelihood - especially if our interpetation of "the persons that they had acquired in Haran" is correct. In that case, Abram was head of a large and successful workforce, willing to take their chances with him as leader.

Preferred parallel cousin marriages, as Abram's and Sarai's, may have been often arranged and do not suggest that their marriage could be called a "love relationship", which in any case failed to produce the expected family.

The Dream as expressed in the call would change all that. The call suggested a connection with a Force, an inner voice, or nameless divinity who would act as teacher, adviser, sponsor, guide - an exemplar who would support and facilitate "the realization of the Dream".

The Dream as expressed in his "Mentor's Formulation" promised a grand, even grandiose compensation for all that has been missing in his novice phase. He will not only have a family, but become a great nation. He will not only be blessed but he shall be loved, honored, "a standard by which blessing is invoked" (J.P.S) "I will make your name great, And you shall be a blessing" (12:2). i.e. be a model for and recipient of many loving relationships. "All the families of the earth shall bless themselves by you" But more, his mentor will ward off and protect him from the destructive narcisstic envy of others[25]: I will bless those who bless you and curse him that curses you. (12:3).

The Dream at this stage seems to have many grandiose and "magical" aspects. During his Mid-Life transition, Abram will have many occasions "to reappraise the magical aspects of the Dream and modify its place in their middle adult lives" yet not abandon the Dream so that "it may simply die, and with it his sense of aliveness and purpose" (Levinson 1978:92). With this newly formulated Dream, however, Abram is ready and willing, to break out and search for a new life structure, in a new place.

When Abram broke away from father, kin and country, he followed a nameless inner voice. He went, in silence, neither believing nor disbelieving the grave and grandiose promises (cf. 15:6). But when he arrived at his destination, he received a vision of recognition that this land was to be the land of destiny. In recognition, "he built an altar there to the Lord who had appeared to him" (12:7). Moving in search of new pastures from "Schechem" (modern Nablus) to "hill country east of Bethel and pitched his tent with Bethel on the west and Ai on the east[26]; he built there an altar to the Lord and invoked the Lord by name" (12:8). These are the first altars built in the Land and the very first revelation in Scripture. What Abram did at the altars or what name Abram used to call his God is unclear (see Appendix "The Name of God"). The text here used the tetragrammaton, YHWH often written in English "Jehovah"or "Yahweh". (Fox 1983) The tradition recorded in Exodus 5:2 claimed that Abram did not know God by this name: "I am Yahweh. To Abraham and Isaac and Jacob I appeared as El Shaddai; I did not make myself known to them by my name Yahweh".

My understanding of "invoked the Lord by name" follows King James version "called upon the name of the Lord" i.e, he called to the God who appeared to him, but he did not yet know his name - or perhaps he did use an epithet, as he later did, "El Elyon" (God Most High), El Olam (Everlasting God) but one that had unacceptable traces of Mesopotamian divinites.

The achievement of a sense of place in his new land was short lived. Drought, faminine and shortage of water are regular aspects of the promised land. Without access to water resources, he could not survive. As in his trek with his father,

Abram now must have been bitterly disappointed in his father-derived God-image (Jung 1961). There is no sense, here, as there is in later narratives, that famine is the result of sin and disobedience (but cf. Ramban) but rather drought as a natural catastrophe, for which continuing migration, moving ever southward through the Negev into Sinai and Egypt is the time tested response. What happened in Egypt, however, is anything but natural.[27] Abram asks his wife to "say you are my sister" (12:13).

Women, Disguise and Birth Order

Women play a crucial role in the family history of the patriarchs. The infertility of the matriarchs is an essential ingredient in the inter-flow of events, human with divine, highlighting each generation's special child of promise. The women are portrayed as strong, indeed often tougher than their men. Witness Sarah ordering Abraham to exile her handmaiden's son; Rebekah conspiring with her son against her husband; Rachel's lament to her husband, "Give me children or I die" (30:1). Hagar comes in for special attention and clearly the God of Abraham is also the God of Hagar and Ishmael. What is missing in Genesis is not the importance of woman but their point of view.[28] How did Sarai feel being taken off to Pharaoh's harem? How did she then resume married sexual life - or did she? How did Sarah react to the 'akeda' or Abraham's marriage to Keturah, which narrative sequence notwithstanding may very well have taken place during her lifetime?

Women, are also experts in disguise. Rebekah, as well as Sarah, play at being her husband's "sister"; Rebekah instructs Jacob how to be like his brother; in the marital bed Leah passes as Rachel (in a counterpoint of the trickster Jacob tricked); Rachel deceives her father by pretending to be menstruating; the strange story of Dinah also involves a bloody deception, and finally, Judah's daughter-in-law Tamar seduces him dressed as a Temple prostitute (Hebrew קדשה). These feminine disguises allow one to acquire by cunning what one cannot achieve by legitimate means.

Most, (though not Sarah's double disguise), involve reversing biological birth order. Being a first born or later born had important legal and psychological implications. In later Law of Moses the first born was awarded a double portion from his father's estate. Moreover this "right of the first-born" was fixed and not subject to paternal judgement (cf. Deut 21:15-17 in which first born of an unloved wife must be acknowledged as first-born).

Egyptian practice as reflected in 48:17-20; 29:26 indicated a clear first-born preference. In Genesis no rule of primogeniture is stated, (but cf. Ch. 27). Rather there seems to be a clear preference of later born over first born, in practice. Adam's first born Cain is disinherited in favor of later born Seth; Abraham's first born Ishmael is disinherited in favor of Isaac; Jacob, the younger twin receives his father's blessing by deceit (and purchase) and he in turn blesses his younger grandson Ephraim (48:19) instead of Joseph's first born saying to Joseph's objections "...his younger brother shall be greater than he..." (48:19). Jacob's own first born Reuben is presumably disqualified of his birthright by improper sexual activities with his father's concubine (35:24). Judah, the pre-eminent later born son is perpetuated through his younger son, Perez (38:38). In practice, despite a formal preference for firstborns, a father might in practice chose which son would inherit his birthright and blessing.

Agricultural communities faced with fixed and limited land resources often practice primogeniture to preserve economic viability of the inheritance. Pastoralists on the other hand often have a more flexibile system of inheritance. One pattern is "ultimogeniture" in which the youngest son inherits the parental flock, after each of the elder sons have been set up in turn on their own. The youngest son remains with his aging parents, caring for them in old age and receving what remains of the parental holdings. Another pattern leaves inheritance to parental discretion. Normally a first son would be chief heir, but if he were unfit or a more talented younger son appear then the first born might be passed over (Wilson 1977). Such a pattern occurred in the Kingdom of Jordan when King Abdullah was assassinated. An unfit son was passed over in favor of his grandson, the present King Hussein.

The ambiguity surrounding inheritance in Genesis reflect, I suggest, the tensions between a more flexible pastoral style of inheritance, in which first-born may be deferred, and a more agrarian mode typical of fixed land holdings, in which the eldest is always preferred. The argument between Abraham and Sarah concerning the disinheritance of Ishmael involves not only a legal clash over the legal standing of a handmaiden's son - can he be a legal heir?- but also apparently over the implicit rule that inheritance is not fixed but subject to parental preference.

Although it is not crucial to our argument, it is probable that Abram was himself not first born son of Terah. Genesis 11:26 does record Terah's sons in the following order: "Abram, Nahor and Haran". However, sons are not always listed in the order of their birth but usually in their order of eminence (Cassuto 1964). In Genesis 10:1 Noah's sons are listed as "Shem, Ham and Japhet" but 9:24 indicates that Ham was "his youngest son" and 10:21 that Shem was "older brother of Japheth"[29]. The birth order, in contrast to the "eminence order" is thus: Shem, Japheth, Ham". Likewise, at the burial of Abraham (25:9), his sons are listed in order of preminence, "Isaac and Ishmael" not in birth order; (cf. also 5:4 in which Adam's third son, Seth, is discussed to the exclusion of his older brothers.)

On the other hand, the **toledot**, the line of Ishmael (25:12-18), is given before the "story of Isaac". Given this narrative principle of listing sons in order of pre-eminence, but giving their **toledot**, in birth order, in narrative sequence[17], then we suggest that Haran was Abram's eldest brother. In narrative sequence Haran's story ("Haran begot Lot, Haran died in the lifetime of his father Terah, in his native land, Ur of the Chaldeans" (11:27-28)) comes before either of his brothers. By a similar logic, Nahor, whose descendants are listed much later (22:20-24) would be the youngest brother who apparently did not have sons when Abram set out from his father's house.

There are, however, other intriguing psychological implications in the first born/later born distinction. (Adler 1956). According to contemporary research,

First-born children are likely to be treated differently from those who are born later...oldest children do not have to share their parents with other children; so they are likely to have a great deal of attention and affection, to have their needs gratified quickly, and to receive help promptly when in distress. They readily learn to depend on and relate to adults. However, to their disadvantage, they may be handicapped by the relative inexperience of their parents...and they alone must face the problem of losing "only child" status...

Studies show that firstborns are generally more likely to identify with their parents and to adopt parental - rather than peer - values and to maintain high standards for themselves. In addition, they are more strongly motivated toward achievement, more affiliative and dependent on others for support, more conforming to authority and to social pressures, more conscientious and prone to feelings of guilt, more concerned with cooperation and responsibility, more inclined to enter occupations involving a parent-surrogate role - such as teacher - and more likely to achieve eminence in their professions.

Compared with firstborns, later-born children are more likely to suffer from feelings of inadequacy, to be more realistic in self-evaluations but less cautious in behavior - for instance, they tend to participate more in dangerous physical activities. In their home, these later-born children learn to consider and to accomodate to the needs and wishes of others, including their siblings and thus acquire many important social skills, These interpersonal skills tend to generalize to other situations, and consequently, their interactions with peers tend to be successful, leading to greater popularity.

...To be first or second, to have great or little power, to side with authority or rebel against it, to feel guilt over hostility or to be able to "place the blame" are tendencies that begin to be differentially strengthened during early childhood as a result of the child's sibling position.

(Mussen, Conger & Kagan 1979:370-72)

Firstborns are therefore, more successful, but more anxious, more pressured to succeed, more tied to parental figures. Laterborns feel less adequate but have better interpersonal skills, more able to take risks; they are more comfortable in a world, which included, from the outset, not only powerful parental figures, but also important older siblings who provide a further dimension of basic security. The danger for firstborns is parental incompetence and "destructive entitlement" (Boszormenyi-Nagy & Krasner 1986), the feeling that "I deserve it" or "I deserve everything and don't need to give in return".

Laterborns are less likely to feel such a destructive entitlement since they enter into a family context in which sharing is a basic given. Laterborns also often have the benefit of firstborns experience and in the case of an unsuccessful eldest, may be able to chose or invent an alternative path.

Firstborns are also "topdogs" just as laterborns are "underdogs". In the collective memory as late comers to the land of Canaan, the Hebrews saw "themselves as perpetual underdogs because of the historical circumstances of their origins" (Niditch 1987:48).

From a theological perspective, the memory of this "younger brother" status as stranger - underdogs - served as a collective restraint to the all-too-real danger of destructive entitlement and narcissistic expectation of specialness.

The interpreter has to know his limitation. Whoever said that everything here must or could be satisfactorily explained?

- *von Rad (1972:169-170)*

Plural Identities: Abram as Husband/Brother

The switching of husband to brother, wife to sister is one of the most puzzling aspects of the story of Abram and Sarai.

The fact that the strategem is repeated three times has led many scholars to suggest that it represents two or three independent traditions which were later amalgamated into the final version. (cf. Niditch 1987) But from the point of view of the text as received it is clear that this wife/sister, husband/brother switch is given strong emphasis. Van Rad (1972:167) calls the narrative "offensive and difficult to interpret". Sarna (1966:102) calls it "one of the strangest of the patriarchal narratives".

In the Appendix on "Patriarchal Culture" I suggested that such strategies of deception were a regular part of the cultural repetoire of the migrant patriarchs, as indeed Abraham says in his spirited defense of the practice to the King of Gerar:

"I thought", said Abraham "Surely there is no fear of God in this place, and they will kill me because of my wife. And besides in truth she is my sister, my father's daughter though not my mother's; and she became my wife. So when God made me wander from my father's house, I said to her, "Let this be the kindness that you shall do me: whatever place we come to, say there of me: He is my brother." (20:11-13).

In the "p'shat", the plain sense of the text, the three recurrences of the "trick" are just that, three occasions in which an underdog-trickster maneuver was successfully utilized.[30] (cf. Appendix)

One meaning of the wife-sister/husband-brother story is that it is a political allegory (Rosenberg 1986), in which the acts of the fathers are a sign to their descendants (Ramban 1972). One political scientist has put is poetically: "Israel as a people is the beautiful woman who is taken by pharaoh until he discovers that she belongs to another, her God, after which she is sent away better off than she came"

(Wildavksky 1984:245, n.41). The second version might then symbolize the second danger of Israel, the still beautiful woman cohabitating with local Canaanite (or Philistine) king and religion, only to be saved by divine and prophetic intervention. Such political allegory, however fascinating, does not help us understand the significance of these events in the life of Abram and Sarai. The fact that Sarai (whose geneology seems deliberately not given) may be a patrilineal half sister or a classificatory sister (i.e. a patrilineal relative such as niece who is called "sister") does not mitigate the Mosiac damnation of these acts. His acts are triply culpable according to the Law of Moses. Leviticus 18:9 specifically prohibits marrying or sexual intercourse with even half sister ("You must not uncover the nakedness of your sister, whether she is your father's or your mother's daughter. Whether she is born in the same house or elsewhere, you must not uncover her nakedness") while Deut. 24:1-4 even more strongly forbids receiving a former repudiated wife after she has been wife of another man ("...her first husband, who has repudiated her, may not take her back as his wife now that she has been defiled in this way. For that is detestable in the sight of Yahweh, and you must not bring guilt on the Land that Yahweh your God gives for your inheritance"). Moreover, Abram initiates his wife's adultery (as well as that of the "other man", Pharaoh, King of Gerar) which according to Deut. 22:22 is a capital offense for those who committ the adultery ("If a man is caught sleeping with another man's wife, both must die, the man who has slept with her and the women herself. You must banish this evil from Israel.") As we see from the Gen 20 version, even the innocent victim may get hurt as the king learns to his horror in a dream: "But God came to Abimelech in a dream by night saying to him, "You are to die because of the women that you have taken, for she is a married woman." (20:3). Avimelech's reply echoes Abraham's cry at the beginning of the Dialogue over Sodom," "O Lord, will You slay people even though innocent? (JPS)/"My Lord, would you kill innocent people, too?"(JB) (20:4) vs. "Will you sweep away the innocent along with the guilty?" (KJ) (18:23) "Are you really going to destroy the just man with the sinner?" reiterating the main theme of moral culpability and universal justice.

The elusive meaning of these stories probably relates to Abram's identity as an underdog (Niditch 1987), an identity he shares with Jacob and the young David. The underdog can trickster-like disguise his identity "in a good cause, where power relationships are assymetrical (cf. the excuses of the midwives about failing to kill Hebrew boys)" (Wildavksy 1984:245, n.41). Compare the underdog disguises of Jacob as his older brother; the disguise of Leah as her younger sister (a variant on wife/sister:wife-as-sisters); the disguise of Tamar to seduce her deceiving father-in-law, Joseph's brothers who disguise their (attempted) murder as death by wild beast and subsequent disguise of Joseph to his brothers hiding behind his Egyptian identity, as if to make the cycle complete. (cf. also Saul disguised as ecstatic prophet or to visit the witch of endor (I Sam 28:8f). David's disguise as a madman at Gath (I Sam 21:13-16 "...he played the madman and when they held him, feigned lunacy. He would drum on the doors of the gate and let his spittle run down his beard. Achish (the king of Gath) said to his servants, "You can see this man is mad. Why bring him to me? Have I not enough madmen without your bringing me this one to weary me with his antics?").

Disguise is part of the underdog's ethic of survival.[31]

Abraham/Abram is not only a underdog but also a trickster (Radin 1956; Edwards 1978; Niditch 1987) "capturing the social and moral dilemmas of people living under condtions of enforced political and economic marginality" (Edwards 1978:72-3 cited in Niditch 1987:49). In Egypt, in Gerar, even at Moriah, "success is achieved in an irregular roundabout way, by deception, a trick". Edwards notes further that trickster tales involve the choice between adopting the value system of the dominant society or "maximizing short-term gain", which is "a dilemma inherent...to an extent in the world of every socialized human being." (op.cit).

Unlike folk heroes of folklore, who remain "gross deceiver, crude prankster creator of earth, a fool caught in his own lies" Abram is a bricolage, an admixture of noble and foolish, heroic and cowardly, daring and deceitful, often beaten but never defeated (Ricketts 1964;65), often a wanderer (Radin 1956). Deceiver, creator, acculurator, unmasked liar - these qualities of the trickster do apply to the deceiving, ethically ambiguous survivor, Abram of Genesis 12:10-20.

The story which gives most contrast to wife/sister is the account of Dina's "rape" and the subsequent massacre of the people of Schechem by her brothers, Shimon and Levi (Ch. 34). As in much of patriarchal history we are not given Dina's point of view in the story and she conveniently disappears from Biblical view. In Dina's case, a woman is raped and the raper falls in love with her and wants to marry her (the contrast to this contrast is clearly the story of the rape of another Tamar, by her half brother Amnon, who rapes her and dispises her; significantly in her attempt to prevent rape she proposes marriage, between half siblings ("Go now and speak to the king; he will not refuse to give me to you" (I Sam. 13:14) indicating that such "incestuous" marriages were allowable at least in the Royal Court).

The narrative background to Dina's rape is similar to Abram's i.e. an endogenous ethnic group, favoring cousin marriage, migrates to a new, potentially dangerous territory. The indigenous inhabitants propose mutual wife exchange (i.e. reciprocal exogamy) to create a unified society based on wife-givers and wife-takers, the sisters of one becoming the wives of the others. Thus Hamor: "Intermarry with us: give us your daughters to us, and take our daughters for yourself" (34:9). The route of intermarriage is a guarantee to residency rights ("the land will be open before you; settle, move about, and acquire holdings in it." (34:10)).

The same arguments are repeated by Hamor to his own in-group when convincing the town's men to become circumcized. But despite this blood gesture, Dina's brothers revenge their sister's honor and take "all their wealth, all their children, and their wives, all that was in the house, they took as captives and booty" (34:29) without giving anything in return. The conclusion of the story, the bitter exchange between Jacob's expedient but genocidal concerns - the Schechmites have been wiped out and he fear the same fate "...if they unite against me and attack me, I and my house will be destroyed" (34:30) and his sons answered "Should our sister be treated like a whore" (34:31) leave the story athrust with moral ambiguity on all sides. Even the locals are not-blameless for in their speech there is a hint that they planned to do the same to the Hebrews at a future convenient moment. cf. "Would not their cattle and substance and all their beasts be ours?" (34:23). The result is the rule that sisters will not be made into stranger's wives but all parties are dishonored (Pitt-Rivers 1977).

In contrast to his great-grandchildren, Simon and Levi, Abram's and later Abraham's trickster deception seems downright benign. Yet, like them he is a wife-giver, with all the benefits and none of the problems. As brother-guardian (cf. the role of Laban to Rebekah), he receives brideprice and residency rights. But he takes no wife for himself from the Egyptians.

He uses an expedient "transient exogamy" to support long-term endogamy. In other words, as a husband-brother, he gets all the advantages of being a wife-giver without being a wife-taker, so that for the short term he has the gain of good ties with local rulers without endangering the purity of his stock or rigid in-group ethnic group boundaries.

The many examples of expedient disguise highlight the dialectic between identity and destiny. If one knows who one is, then expedient disguise, pretending to be other than who you really are, is acceptable since it furthers one's destiny. Destiny is the best guardian of one's true identity. Destiny requires survival. Faced between the choice between destiny and truth, between survival and saying who you really are, choose disguise. The trickster motto becomes: Disguise and survive.

But what was the meaning of such "role reversals" for Abram (and Sarai!) in their adult development. From a pragmatic point of view, Abram must be close to convinced that he would never have children by Sarai his wife. On the other hand as a "sister" or close paternal kin, divorce was probably out of the question - an alternative which otherwise might have be seemed attractive. The text clearly suggests that she was "taken" ("When When Abram entered Egypt, the Egyptians saw how very beautiful the woman was. Pharaoh's courtiers saw her and praised her to pharaoh and the woman was taken into pharaoh's palace" (12:15) - rather than "given" by her "brother". The text and at least some ancient records suggest that Abram's fear was not groundless i.e. without godfearing attitude, men would easily kill a husband to take a very beautiful women for pharaoh. Yielding Sarai to pharaoh was an almost honorable way of ridding himself of his infertile wife. How Sarai felt about this arrangement is something the text does not reveal.

The ease with which Abram and Sarai switch from husband and wife to brother and sister further suggests that their marriage was in a state of marital breakdown, in that they were more like siblings than lovers. Indeed, one common cause of psychogenic impotence (which clearly affects Abram before the birth of Isaac cf. 17:17 "Can a child be born to a man a hundred years old...; 18:12 "...am I to have enjoyment with my husband so old?") is that wife is felt to be a mother or sister. If Abram felt toward Sarai as towards a sister[32], then sex would be psychologically "incest" leading to psychogenic impotence. Moreover, the absence of sexual jealousy on the part of Abram might be minimal if he felt only like a brother toward Sarai.

There is, however, a deeper meaning in the wife/sister switch. It is the beginning of a repetitive pattern, which lasts through much of Abraham's mid-life transition. It is the pattern of denial (and subsequent reaffirmation) of family ties. Abram first leaves father and kindred, now in Egypt he separates (temporarily) from his wife; upon his return to Cannaan he takes leave of Lot, who settles in Sodom; later he will impregnante his wife's handmaiden, Hagar but she will flee the camp, only to be driven out with the young Ishmael after Isaac's weaning; Sarah will be taken by another king and finally Isaac will be offered up at Mt. Moriah. Taken together, one sees in "Father Abraham" a systematic rejection or detachment from each one of his closest kin!

And why? The spiritual revolutionary in his phase as "lonely man of faith" must be singleminded in his devotion to his cause and his God - not even family ties may deter him. Thus the detachment from kin. But since Abraham's vision is a spiritual vision for his lineal descendants, then the devotion must be impressed on his children-disciples, hence the repeated cycle of rejection and reaffirmation. In practice, with Sarai in the pharaoh's palace harem, Abram was left free to pursue new religious experiences.[33]

Finally, if we consider the creation of the first man and the first woman from a strict kinship point of view, we discover that the first couple were also patrilineal half siblings, like Abram and Sarai, brother-husband and sister-wife. In a literal sense, they share a divine father but have different mothers. Adam's mother is "adama"; Eve's "mother" is "Adam" - who unconsciously, bisexually gives birth to a feminine partner.

This unconscious incestuous descent may help explain why the theme of incest repeats itself in the book of Genesis.

Abraham as Mentor

Levinson has written about the importance of the mentor who "is ordinarily several years older, a person of greater experience and seniority in the world the young man is entering" (Levinson 1977:97). The mentor acts as teacher, sponsor, host and guide, as well as an exemplar for his protegé. "The mentor has another function, and this is developmentally the most crucial one: to support and facilitate the 'realization of the Dream'. The true mentor, in the meaning intended here, serves as an analogue in adulthood of the 'good enough' parent for the child. He fosters the young adult's development by believing in him, sharing the youthful Dream and giving it his blessing, helping to define the newly emerging self in its newly discovered world, and creating a space in which the young man can work on a reasonably satisfactory life structure that contains the dream." (p.98-99).

We know very little about the mentoring which Abram may have received. It is possible that Melchizedek, the king of Salem, may have acted in this fashion but it seems unlikely. Perhaps during his travels to Egypt he did have occasion to experience such a relationship and certainly in a metaphorical fashion, God was truely his mentor: teacher, guide, sponsor, facilitating the realization of the Dream.

We do have more information about Abram as a mentor to other young men, which would be an appropriate developmental role within the mid-life transition. Within the tribal family Abram would not have occasion to mentor strangers but only family members. His first mentee is the son of his dead brother, his nephew Lot.

Abram takes Lot with him from Haran to Canaan, perhaps to Egypt[34] through the Negev to Bethel. Without progeny, Lot as his closest male relative would be his natural heir and therefore the relation of uncle to nephew, like that subsequently of father to son is also that of mentor-mentee. With less invested in Lot as spiritual heir, Abram is willing to effect a magnanimous compromise to avoid an open break with Lot: "Let there be no strife between you and me, between my herdsman and yours, for we are kinsman. Is not the whole land before you? Let us separate" (13:8-9).

Such magnanomous conclusion to a mentoring relationship is not common. Rather it is difficult to terminate such relationships in a reasonable civil manner. With Lot, it ends with a gradual loss of personal involvement, for although Abram has dealings with Lot, twice rescuing him, Scripture records no further conversation between the two men. "Most often, however, an intense mentor relationship ends with strong conflict and bad feelings on both sides. The young man may have powerful feelings of bitterness, rancor, grief, abandonment, liberation and rejuvenation" (Levinson 1978:100). Levinson does not discuss the mentor relation from the point of view of the mentor, who may feel parallel feelings of bitterness and liberation.

Levinson suggests that a mentor is ideally half-generation (8-15 years) older than his protege. When the gap is greater then the relationship tends to be symbolized in parent-child terms, activating powerful feeling, "such as excessive maternalism or paternalism in the elder and dependency or Oedipal conflicts in the younger, that interfere with the mentoring function" (Levinson 1978:99). On the other hand a good mentor combines the good qualities of good father and friend - just as a bad mentor combines the worst features of both. Since, Levinson argues that mentoring is a form of loving, generative relationship, "its ending is often painful" (Levinson 1978:334).

The break of the mentoring relation with Lot came before there was an open break, a wise response to the dangers of overgrazing. The narrative flow concerning the separation implies that in addition to overt cause of the strife, quarreling between their herdsman, there is a latent cause for strife in their relationship with the indiginous inhabitants, the Canaanites and Perizzites.

When Abram first arrived the text states (12:6) "The Canaanites were then in the land". Now after returning from Egypt and the Negev, the Canaanites are joined by another ethnic group, the Perizzites. Two possibilites suggest themselves. First that during Abram's absence, another ethnic group entered the Land, as had Abram and Lot. The arrival of additional populations complicated the local ethnic mix and put greater pressure on the ecology of the land. The quarreling seems to be set in the context of a new and fluid ethnic tensions between newcomers and oldtimers.

A second more benign option is that when Abram first passed through the land of Canaan, he was aware only of the dominant ethnic group, the Canaanites, when he returned he had a more textured view of ethnic differences among the locals he had assumed were all homogenious.

De Vaux (1978) state that if Perizites is a Semitic term, it may mean "those who live in the country as opposed to the city" (P.139 n.54) and according to Lapp (1968), may have been semi-nomads like Abram and Lot, fighting for the same ecological niche. It is significant that after the massacre at Shechem, Jacob refers to "the inhabitants of the land, the Canaanites and the Perizzites, my men are few in nunber, so that if they unite against me and attack me, I and my house will be destroyed" (34:30-31).

Likewise in the beginning of the Book of Judges, Judah and Simon rout 10,000 Canaanites and Perizzites, led by Adoni-zedek (literally from - "zedek" Hebrew for "just" or "justice" hence "Lord of justice"; cf. Melchizedek lit. "King of justice".)

There are 16 other references to the Perizzites in the Bible, in none of them does the term appear alone, but always as part of a list of indigenous ethnic groups such as the list at the close of the vision in Gen. 15:20 which is the most extensive list - 10 names, instead of more usual seven. What is also unusual is that in most lists, Perizites are toward the end of the list, followed by Hivi (Hurrian?) and Jebushi (who lived around Jerusalem); nor are the lists standardized.[35]

In all the lists, Perrizite is a secondary tribe. It joins in the grand alliance to fight Joshua, and like other tribes (Amori, Hivit, Jebusi), occupy the hill country (Joshua 11:3) as well as forested region (Jos 17:15), while the Canaanites are urban population living in the plains. Perizzites are also among the various groups (Hittite, Amori, Perizzite, Hivite, Jebusite) "who were not exterminated by the Israelis but were levied for forced labor... these Solomon conscipted as slave laborers, as they are still" (I Kings 9:20-23; II Chronicles 8:7-9). The upshot is that Perizzites were likely a new ethnic force in Canaan, occupying a formerly less populated hill country; when Abram and Lot returned they found their previous ecological niche, in the hill country now occupied (perhaps it had been temporarily depopulated during the first famine, which caused Abram to himself leave). Such population pressures led to greater competition for grazing land and water resources (cf. Gen 21:25; 26:15, 20-22) and ultimately the break between Abram and Lot.

Wandering Together, Wandering Alone

A time of extreme isolation and deprivation began for Abram. When he left the land of Mesopotania he did not join a new ethnic group but became more or less associated with a new social class of people known as "Hapiru"[36]: he became a man without a country, under no one's protection but his own, an isolated wanderer with no civil or social rights.

The Hapiru were strangers to settled civilization. To become a Hapiru "meant to break one's ties, to leave - at times to flee - one's native land" (Mazar 1967:201) They were fugitive and footloose herders often united in loose bands in a common search for water and pasture and plunder, but with no coherent identity of their own. These uprooted and propertyless persons often threatened the established political order as fighting men, either as mercenaries or as independent groups of raiders. But an individual Hapiru - and Abram would probably have been considered such - was often treated as a vagrant: he was an isolated wanderer living outside the protection of society, the "marginal man", spiritually and socially vulnerable.

Abram's new role as a Hapiru is perhaps indicated in the name he acquired; עברי "ivri," that is, "the Hebrew," Not all Hapiru were Hebrews, but the Hebrews may have been assimilated into the social class "hapiru". In contrast, the Rabbinical tradition has provided two interpretations of the word "Hebrew": one is genealogical, indicating that Abram was descended from Eber, his grandfather's great-grand-father; Eber and "iver" share the same consonantal roots. The other derives "ivri" from the root meaning "to cross over," making Abram the Hebrew, Abram "the one who had crossed over." This crossing refers literally to the crossing of the Euphrates River. In his first journey from Ur to Kharan Abram had travelled the length of the Euphrates without actually ever crossing over it. Crossing a river is of course suggestive spiritually as well as geographically; in crossing over into Canaan and becoming a Hebrew, Abram explored new physical space and discovered new spiritual territory as well.

But if his social identity had now become so fixed, his personal identity had become more flexible. As an outsider he was unconstrained by formality or social convention; as a wanderer he was free to come and go as he chose. He thus became free to pursue a personal identity more authentic than the one he had left behind in Kharan. He was able to develop his own strengths and resources, and become self-reliant.

As a first step in realising his self-reliance Abram would have had to shed his urban ways. (Wooley 1936; Parrott 1956; Albright 1963). Throughout **Genesis** - and indeed in all scripture - city life and city people were generally associated with evil, beginning with Cain, who built the first city (4:27).

Finally Abram, having repeatedly demonstrated his readiness to give up all to follow the urgings of his inner Voice, was now commanded to do precisely that: leave all behind and explore his promised land alone. He therefore left Sarai behind and spent about a period in isolation, travelling the limits of the land. Returning in the end to Hebron, Abram reaffirmed his affiliation with Yahweh, built his third altar and settled down.

This period of isolation marked the initiation of the second phase in his spiritual development. The first phase had been his wandering and initial exposure to new existential and religious experiences. This second phase, a period of intense and extreme isolation, is often a necessary experience in the lives of great religious innovators, Moses in the Midian desert, Jesus in the Judean wilderness, Muhammed in the cave near Mecca, Gautama under the Bo tree, each experienced an intense period of extreme suffering and despair in which, undistracted by family obligations and practical concerns of daily living, they were able to turn deeply inward to assimilate the elements of their experience and discover the extent of their vision and resources. For the chosen few, this "dark night of the soul" culminated in a direct experience of the shining luminance of the whole vision.

Abram's need for this kind of intense isolation supports Toynbee's notion that creative response to ecological or psychological challenge follows a pattern of withdrawal or isolation, a turning inward to discover one's depth, the ultimate foundation of one's resources. Then, having made the breakthrough, the visionary returns to share the fruits of the vision with society or to transform the very nature of human relations. In so doing, according to Erikson's hypothesis, an extraordinary individual like Abram manages to solve for others, dilemmas which he was unable to resolve for himself alone.

CHAPTER FIVE:
ABRAM THE FOUNDER

Abraham the Warrior

Genesis 14 stands alone in Genesis and perhaps in all Biblical literature. The narrative style and vocabulary are distinct. It presents a historical perspective different from the rest of the Abraham narrative. The focus shifts suddenly from details of Abram's personal life to the imperial politics of the Ancient Near East - suddenly Abram's actions are placed on a world stage of international politics, warfare and diplomacy. Moreover, there is an irony in that he is able to rescue a kinsman from an army from his own abandoned homeland. But for the would be historian, this chapter is a temptation and a nightmare:

Probably no chapter of Scripture has been so thoroughly studied as Genesis 14. It is a notoriously seductive chapter, tantalizing the scholar with a real name here, and a seemingly historical name there. Nevertheless, the search for a solution has not abated, as is attested by an unceasing flow of articles and monographs.

In spite of some rough spots in composition, Genesis 14 reads as a relatively organic whole. The war was a necessary backdrop to the heroic deeds of Abraham, who as a warrior, allied by pact with Lot, Aner, Eshkol and Mamre, with his 318 troops in number, restores not only the plundered goods of Lot but those of his allies as well. Decisive in battle yet noble in peace, Abraham refuses to take a share in booty - neither property nor slaves, neither string nor sandal-lace - his only concern being the rations of his troops and a legitimate share for his allies (Muffs 1980:81-2: cf. also Van Seters 1975; van Rad 1972; Sarna 1966; Hallo & Simpson 1971).

In our discussion, we make no attempt to link up with historicity of Abram or the four Kings (Thompson 1974). From internal evidence, one can state with certainty that the present form of the chapter was composed after the Book of Judges. In Genesis 14:14 Abram chases Chedorlaomer's troops "as far as Dan". Dan was origially called Leshem (Joshua 19:47) or Laish (Judges) prior to the migration of the tribe of Dan as described in Judges 18:28-31:

... the Danites marched against Laish, against a peaceful and trusting nation,
They slaughtered all the inhabitants and set the town on fire. There was no
one to help the town because it was a long way from Sidon and no relations
with the Aramaeans. It lay in the valley running toward Beth-rehob. They
rebuilt the town and settled in it, and called it Dan after Dan their father who
had been born to Israel, although the town was originally called Laish.

Since Genesis 14 does not, as in other cases, cite the original names, one can
assume that the audience knew these places as Dan, indicating that the chapter was
written at a later period.

Chapter 14 has strong parallels to Chapter 19. In both, Abraham attempts to
rescue the Sodomites, in both, he has been or is about to be made rich; not by the
King of Sodom but by his wife; in both he gets and gives recognition from a local
authority, the King of Salem or the King at Gerar. The events take place against a
cultural background of Patriarchal Culture. Abram and Lot as "kinsmen" or "brothers"
share collective sense of responsibility. An attack on one is also an attack on the
other; the sins of one may be the responsibility of his relatives. The phrase, "When
Abram heard his kinsman had been taken captive..." (14:14) appropriately emphasizes
the social bond, not the personal bond between them. Abraham must rescue his
kinsman, no matter what he may think of Lot. The theme of "collective responsibility"
is reiterated in 18:23f and is a major element of the Biblical sense of "justice within
community".

Abram's success is "a daring but largely inconsequential night raid" i.e. he did
not take on the entire army but only the bagage train with Lot "his possessions, and
the women and the rest of the people" (14:16). His concern over spoils is also
related in turn to ancient pattern of division of booty and Hittite treaty-making.
(Muffs 1980).

But for our purposes, the success of the raid won social recognition and protection
from the local authorities. Melchizedek (lit, "My King is Just"), King of Salem
(traditionally identified with Jeru-salem; "salem" perhaps cognate to "peace" or
"whole") greets the victor with a symbolic or possibly ritual meal of "bread and
wine" (14:18) - which remain the basic sacraments of Biblical Religion.

Melchizedek is called a priest of "El Elyon" and he blesses the victor:

Blessed be Abram of God Most High (El Elyon)
Creator of heaven and earth
And blessed be God Most High,
Who has delivered your foes into your hands.

Melchizedek remains a mysterious figure. But if he did function as a religious mentor, his role was to fuse a Creator God, like, the Canaanite, El, with a God who guides history, and the personal guardian of a clan. Theologians have criticized him for praising Abram before God Most High; but it is clear that Abram, is willing to grant him a tithe ("a tenth of everything" 14:20) in exchange for the recognition. Melchizedek's ploy, contrasts sharply with that of the rescued King of Sodom. His phrase, "Give me the persons, and take the possessions for yourself" (14:21) has been understood usually as manipulative - since the persons could easily be held for ransom. But I prefer to interpret his speech and Abram's sharp rejoinder: "I swear (lit. "lift up my hand") to the Lord, God Most High, Creator of Heaven and Earth: I will not take so much as a thread or a sandal strap of what is yours; you shall not say,'It is I who made Abram rich'" (14:22-4) otherwise. Apparently by rights of the law of war and the division of spoils (cf. I Sam 30), Abram is entitled to both persons and possessions as well as provisions for his allies. The King of Sodom however, is trying to reframe the situation by giving Abram his spoils as a "gift" - and it is the implications of such a gift which Abram is quick to avoid. Gift-giving is a form of social exchange which reinforces a social bond. Receiving a gift in some way makes one beholden to the gift-giver. Between equals, receiving a gift usually implies that one will on the appropriate occasion reciprocate; between unequals, gifts are expressions of anticipated favors. By refusing the King of Sodom's offer, Abram declines to enter into such a "gift- exchange" relationship. Abram will not end up, even indirectly beholden, to the Sodomites, whose name will soon become the Biblical byword for immorality. On the other hand, Abram's speech shows how much he learned from Melchizedek. He now uses the phrase, "Lord, God Most High, Creator of Heaven and Earth", a decisive step away from God, as a father-image, to that of a transcendent, ethically concerned Creator. His actions show his moral superiority to both the run of the mill "hapiru" and especially the King of Sodom. Moreover, Abram added the personal name יהוה YHWH, here translated as "Lord" to Melchizedek's rhetorical innovation, showing his political alliance yet spiritual independence. This confrontation was Abram's first public invocation of his special relationship to the locally unknown Deity, YHWH. No mention is made of any communication between him and Lot at this or any future time. The implication is that the break between uncle and nephew was final, the moral and economic gulf separating Abram's pastoral and Lot's urban-merchant's life was unbridgeable. Although many commentators interpret Abraham's second defense of Sodom (18:22f) as a personal defense of Lot, no mention is made of Lot during Abraham's bargaining over the fate of Sodom.

The final separation from Lot meant that Abram had no biological kin within his growing camp. Indeed, it is possible he made use of ritual adoption of a servant,

"Damesek Eliezer", in order to act as his heir in order to preform funeral rites as occurred in some Mesopotamian societes (De Vaux 1978; Sarna 1966; Livingston 1987). His political, economic and social success throw into harsh perspective his lack of any real sense of biological continuity. As he climbs the ladder, during mid-life transition, he must continually ask, "What am I really getting out of all this seeming success?"

Failure forces a person to confront the inadequacies of his or her life structure, to modify and restructure the Dream. But success, no less than failure may disrupt the life structure, when advancement itself produces a change. Levinson describes the basic pattern as follows:

> *A man recieves a promotion or a drastic increase in income. At first glance the increase seems to be a great boon, an opportunity to live better and do things that he has long wanted to do. But this gain propels him into a new world in which he has new roles and relationships. It activates new aspects of the self, while providing little room for the expression of other formerly important aspects. In short, it leads to a change in his life structure. The advancement is a mixed blessing, and it may turn out to be a curse. (Levinson, 1978:160-1)*

After such success, a man is driven to ask, "What next?" For Abram, at this juncture in his unfolding life history, his material successes are pitted against his spiritual failure of being, a "non-father", cut off from an ongoing sense of the continuity of life.

What follows in Genesis 15 is one of the strangest and most intimate chapters in Scripture. It depicts a dialogue in words and ritual, between a man and his God, set against this tragic background of material success and spiritual-biological failure.

The Revelation of Innumerable Stars

"After these things", when God speaks,

Fear not, Abram,
"I am a shield to you
Your reward shall be great (15:1)

Abram does not remain silent but responds:

0 Lord God, what can You give me, seeing that I die childless...(15:1-2).

God's, reassurances, presumably have to do with the military dangers and magnanomous dispensation of Gen. 14[37] - Abram might have been killed; he gave up blood revenge, the spoils of battle. But the soothing words, echoed in daily Jewish prayer, "Blessed is God, the shield of Abraham" do not address Abram's "project" (Sartre 1953), of paternity; an "image of ultimate horror" intrudes - that a "stranger", "the one in charge of my household"[38] will inherit him.

Besides verbal reassurance, "That one shall not be your heir, none but your very own issue shall be your heir" (15:4) - What does the Lord do to reassure Abram? He takes him outside and shows him "the stars" saying, "Look toward heaven and count the stars, if you are able to count them." This act recalls the covenant of the rainbow (9:12-17)[39] a natural phenomena which is an everlasting sign of the bond between God and Man. The rainbow, however, is a sign for **God**: "When the bow is in the clouds, I will see it and remember the everlasting covenant between God and all living creatures, all flesh that is on earth" (9:16). But the rainbow[40] was also a sign to "all living things" which signaled that the flood, that "image of ultimate horror" (Lifton 1979:172) would never come again.

Likewise, stars are a natural symbol of wonder and hope, precious commodities in "middle age". They are likewise symbols of a divine promise an "image of ultimate hope" to counter the personal image of ultimate horror of Abraham viz. to die childless (Hebrew: ariri), to be "cut off". Although astronomers claim that there are a finite number of observable stars in the night sky - about 4,000 can be seen without telescope - the celestial field is in constant if slow motion, so stars disappear and appear as one is counting: a "natural symbol" of the succession of generations. Stars, like grains of the sand on the seashore (22:17), become a perennial, accessible image of innumerability: descendants without end, a visual image of "symbolic biological immortality" (Lifton 1979).

Watching the innumerable stars, the J.P.S. translation of the text states, "And because he put his trust in the Lord, He reckoned it to his merit"[41] (following the commentator, Rashi). Another interpreter, Ramban, however, rejects this translation asking, what merit was due Abram for believing such a delightful prophecy. Rather he argued, it is Abram who reckoned the promises to God's merit, as so the K.J. translation reflecting the ambiguity of the pronouns in the original, where "he" might be "He" and "him", "Him": "he counted it to him for righteousness". (15:6)

If the latter translation is correct, as I believe, it indicates that Abram has developed an autonomous internalized morality, one of the threshold of becoming a moral authority in his own right, soon able to go on to judge God Himself.

Having one natural symbol for innumerable progeny, he asks for another "image of ultimate hope" for inheriting the land: "How shall I know that I am to possess it?" (15:8). Abram, it seems, is not expressing doubt - he had already done so (15:2) - but asking for a visual image[47] as a sign, as the uncounted stars of heaven had for the heir "of your own flesh and blood" (J.B.).

What follows is a form of covenant sacrifice, the ritual affirmation of a transpersonal relationship between Abram, his descendants and God.

Until this pivotal encounter of the seven theophanies Abram had only **heard** his "Voice", now he had a directed "Vision".[43] The move from auditory to visual mode of communication reflect his newfound intimacy with his Lord, meeting as it is said of Moses, "face to face". No longer is this a relationship patterned on father-son, authority-compliance, but one of growing mutuality and values shared.

"From Life History to Life Story"

The dramatic revelation:

> *'I am the Lord who brought you out from Ur of the Chaldeans to give you this land as a possession*

(15:7)

is full of paradox. This is the first time in the text that God speaks using the tetragrammaton, the four letter word for God, YHWH (usually pronounced "Jehova" or "Yahweh") and in the next verse, Abram addresses Him as "my Lord YHWH". Yet the priestly tradition of Exodus 6:3 states God did not make Himself known to the fathers, Abraham, Isaac and Jacob by this Name, only by El Shaddai:

> *To Abraham and Isaac and Jacob I appeared as El Shaddai; I did not make myself known to them by my name Yahweh* (J.B.)

"El Shaddai" is traditionally rendered "God Almighty" (J.P.S.) or "Almighty God" (K.J.), although the meaning has not yet been explained satisfactorily' (van Rad 1976:198). It is an "ancient name of God" occuring frequently in Job and in Genesis (28:3; 35:11; 43:14; 48:3; 49:25), perhaps wedding a Canaanite term "El" with a Mesopotamian "Shaddai".

Was the tradition of Exodus 6:3 unaware of the revelation of Genesis 15:17? Did the redactor fail to observe the contradiction in the passages or did he deliberately insert God's name as Yahweh to make Moses "misunderstand"[44] God? One passage echoes the other: "God spoke to Moses and said to him, "I am Yahweh...I will bring you ("hotzeiti") out of the burdens laid on by the Egyptians...to the land I swore that I would give to Abraham..." (Ex. 6:2,6,8). Remembering that Biblical Hebrew verbs have no tense, but only completed or incompleted action, the form "hotzeti" can mean both "I did bring" and "I will bring", both definite completed actions.[45] The structualist paradigm suggests the equivalence of Ur and Egypt, both places of slavery, from which God **will** as He surely **did** bring Abraham, Moses and the Hebrew people to the land of promise. "El Shaddai" and "Yahweh" are equated; but for Moses, there is a clear historical message: the patriarchal religious experience, the revelation of the fathers, was different from his own, i.e. Moses' encounter is different from the ancestral theophany of Abraham, Isaac and Jacob.

The point of the parallelism and the reiteration of the promise (despite the differing names of God), is that the God of Abraham, call him Yahweh, call him El Shaddai, does not forget!

But there is a second paradox. The text of 11:31 stated that it was Abram's father, Terah, who using the verb of power and authority, "took" Abram from Ur. Now Abram is told the Lord (Yahweh) did it. If we recall that Terah set out originally intending to come to Canaan, we begin to discern a subtle change, a restructuring of Abram's life. At the time when he was taken from Ur, Abram felt his father was taking him out; now he learns, retrospectively, it was the Lord who was guiding his way even then. Such a change in point of view is not a rewriting of personal history, but part of the ongoing process of constructing and re-constructing a lifestory out of a life history (Erikson 1975).

A "lifehistory" is the chronological sequence of a man's marker events; a life story is a personal interpretation of one's life history, which makes a "story" out of the fragments. In a sense, the life story is always imposed on a life history, in retrospect. As we are living our life, we are often overwhelmed by choices, which appear especially during transitional periods. It is as if we come to an intersection with many different pathways. Having selected one path, whether by chance, impulse or foresight, we link up this choice point to the main highway of previous choices to make the meanderings of one's life history become embued with unity and meaning, "This is where my life was always leading me" changing it into a direct story line.

During stable periods we are able to tell coherent life stories to ourselves and to others.[46] During the beginning of transitional periods, the life story breaks down, at least to ourselves. The Life Story becomes fragmented, incomplete, wrong; the "happy ending" is missing. A life history can loose its consistency, its sense of what "my life is all about". At the end of the transition in the move to the following stable period e.g. Middle Adulthood, once again, one is able to literally re-construct a life story he can tell himself and to others. (Abramovitch 1986).

In telling Abram that He took him out of Ur, The Lord is giving Abram's life history the sense of a life story. In taking Terah's place, God is creating a place for Himself in Abram's life story. God was always with Abram, a hidden but guiding force, watching over him, and his destiny. In this sense it represents a development in Abram's "God-image". The God of the Call (12:1-6) I suggested was a God, very much in his father's image. Abram's response, silent obedience without inner conviction, typifies that of a child or young adolescent. During the Mid-Life transition Abram has matured, now he is ready for a changed relation with his God.

"To Cut a Covenant"

"The peculiar Hebrew phrase "to cut a covenant" is derived from the practice of severing animals as the seal of a treaty" (Sarna 1966:126). Abraham and Avimelech, King of Gerar, swear a solemn treaty of "friendship" (or al least non-aggression) by "cutting a covenant" of sheep and oxen (21:27). But the so called "covenant between the pieces" is a peculiar and ancient variation on the normal pattern.[47] In this case, the dominant superior party passes between the severed pieces of the animals. In the extra Biblical examples, it is generally believed that "if the contracting party break his oath, he would suffer the same fate" (De Vaux 1978:450). But in Gen 15 "only God bound Himself to a solemn obligation, the patriarch having been the passive beneficiary" (Sarna 1966:126).

The only other Biblical parallel to such a covenant sacrifice is in Jeremiah 43:8-22. That sacrifice, which concerned a sacred ceremony of liberation of slaves in Jerusalem during the time of King Zedekiah, is a promise on which his nobles later reneged. When it came to the attention of Jeremiah, the prophet announced the fate of the perfidious nobles in the name of Yahweh:

And these men who have infringed my covenant, who have not observed the terms of the covenant made in my presence, I will treat these men like the calf they cut in two to pass between the parts of it. As for the nobles of Judah and of Jerusalem, the eunuchs and the priests and all the people of the country who have passed between the parts of the calf, I will put them into the power of their enemies and into the power of men determined to kill them: their corpses will feed the birds of heaven and the beasts of the earth...I am going to make an uninhabited desert of the towns of Judah (J.B.)

The link between the passage in Jeremiah and in Genesis 15 lies not only in the cut covenant sacrifice but in the terrifying image of a "bad death", birds feeding on an unburied corpse. Whereas the nobles of the king are soon to meet their unburied fate at the hands of invaders, Abram, in contrast is described as chasing away the birds of prey from the animal sacrifice, a role he shares with the strange famine time rite of the Gibeonites. There, seven sons of Saul were put to death in the first day of the barley harvest and only one of Saul's wives, Rizpah "did not allow the birds of heaven to come at them by day nor the wild beasts at night" (cf. II Sam 21). This act, I believe, is a symbolic ceremonial struggle between a "religious perspective" and a "common sense" one (cf. Ortner 1974, Geertz 1973). The religious perspective is one in which the ultimate reality of death is denied through reference to a sacred order that transcends everyday experience (Danforth 1982:32). The common sense view asserts, "death is final", as the Baka Pygmies of Cameroons say: "When you're dead, you're dead and that's the end of you" (Woodburn in Block and Parry 1982:195). Abram (or Rizpah), in chasing away the birds[48] is mimetically chasing away the threat of the "common sense" perspective, acting out the triumph over the "natural" fate of man as animal. There is nothing more "natural" than vultures eating corpses, but this image is the antithesis to a religious perspective in which the fate of men and animals are sharply differentiated.

The Mid-life transition, Levinson argues, raises the issues of a man's legacy, his generativity, i.e. "What he passes on to future generations...in his mind it defines to a large degree the ultimate value of his life - and his claim to immortality" (op. cit. p. 218). Levinson goes on: "The desire for an immortalizing legacy is a powerful, "normal" human urge. It stems from the wish for omnipotence and the archetypes of the Young and the Self as eternal figures. This desire can have destructive consequences if it grows, unchecked, into overly elaborate magical forms, as in the Faust legend. On the other hand, if it is nipped in the bud by early failure and disappointment, it may lead to a loss of belief in the self and a denial that anything in the world is worth bequeathing a legacy to." (p.221)
The sacrifice of pieces brings Abram in confrontation with another of the polarities which are central to the developmental tasks of middle adulthood: destruction/creation. The final resolution of this polarity is developed through the destruction of the cities of the Plain (18-19) and Abraham's resulting survivor mission and ultimately in the "akeda" (22). But it begins here:

> *He brought Him all these (offerings) and cut them in two, placing each half opposite the other; but he did not cut up the bird. Birds of prey came down upon the carcass and Abram drove them away. As the sun was about to set, a deep sleep ("tardema") fell over Abram, and a great dark dread descended upon him. (15:10-12).*

During this "dark night of the soul" Abram comes into contact with images of death, destruction and mortality. Levinson writes that the "developmental task is to understand more deeply the place of destructiveness in his own life and in human affairs generally. Much of the work upon this task is unconscious" (Levinson 1977:223-4).
It is worthy of note that the Hebrew תרדמה "tardema" is used only here and to describe Adam during the creation of "a woman" from his rib:

So the Lord God cast a deep sleep ("tardema") upon the man and he slept; and he took one of his ribs and closed up the flesh at that spot. And the Lord God fashioned into a woman the rib He had taken from the man, and He brought her to the man...
Hence a man leaves his father and mother and clings to his wife, so that they will become one flesh (2:21-24).

By association, then, "tardema" is a creative unconscious process. What is born out of Abram, beside the belief in a biological heir, is a "tragic sense of life", the vision of exile and exodus, oppression and redemption for his descendants (15:13-14) relief for his personal death anxiety (15:15) and the seeds of a universal moral order and ethical interpretation of history.[49](15:26):

Know well that your offspring shall be strangers in a land not theirs, and they shall be ensalved and oppressed for four hundred years; but I will execute judgement on the nation they shall serve, and in the end they shall go free with great wealth. As for you,
You shall go to your fathers in peace
You shall be buried at a ripe old age, And they shall return here in fourth generation, for the iniquity of the Amorites is not yet complete. (15:13-16).

This covenant highlights the ethical dichotomy in the relation of Abraham and his descendants, to the land promised to them:

Israel's acquisition of the land is permanent, rooted in ancestral purchases, treaties and cults, and in unsolicited divine promises.

Israel's acquisition of the land is contingent upon Israel's fluctuating worthiness (like all other nations of Canaan) before God. (Rosenberg 1986:87).

The reason for the Egyptian interlude is to allow for the "contingent" option to come to fulfilment, giving Israel, the ethical advantage. The same theme is reiterated again during the God's monologue concerning the fate of Sodom ("For I have singled him out, that he may instruct his children and his posterity to keep the way of the Lord by doing what is right and just, in order that the Lord may bring about for Abraham what He has promised him" (18:19); Avimelech's dream ("Will you slay people even though innocent" (20:4); the expulsion of Ishmael (..."for the son of that slave shall not share in the inheritance with my son Isaac. The matter distressed Abraham greatly, for it concerned a son of his" (21:10-ll) and the akeda ("Now I know that you fear God...(22:12)...because you have done this thing...Your descendants shall seize the gates of their foes...22:16-17). Perhaps Abram's question: "How shall I know that I am to possess it?" and "a great dark dread" which descended upon him were all reflections of the ethical ambiguity of possessing a land which belonged to some other nation - a dilemma which in its "atrocity producing situations" (Lifton 1971) and potential for irresolvable strife has persisted "unto this very day".

Modifying the Marriage

Many men are able to consider seriously in their late thirties and early forties marital problems that they previously ignored or only dimly acknowledged (Levinson 1978:256). Such a process of what Levinson has called "modifying the marriage" appears to have occurred to both Abram and Sarai. The issue of childlessness has become acute for both of them, and when Abram is 86, the equivalent of early forties, the couple faces the probability that they will remain infertile. Sarai proposes an apparently well known custom of "surrogate motherhood" via her handmaiden, evidenced in legal documents from the Ancient Near East (de Vaux 1978; Sarna 1966). But such an arrangement fails to bring the couple together even before the "first promised son" is born. What is worthy of note in the Hagar narratives which follow is that the God of Abram is very much the god of Hagar as he is the god of Ishmael, indicating the decisive move from a family god to a Universal Presence.

The theme of reproductive envy and competition[50] remains an important theme in the woman in the Bible. Besides Sarai, one might mention Rachel and Leah, via their handmaidens and then more directly; Tamar, who acts to seduce her father-in-law out of a need for children; Hanna, whose story is perhaps most moving, and includes a feminist innovation of silent direct prayer as a new mode of private communion.

It is possible that Abram and Sarai settled into a "cold peace". Nowhere it is said of Abraham and Sarah, as it is of Isaac, that "he took Rebeccah as his wife. Isaac loved her..." (24:67). The few direct encounters recorded by Scripture are hardly loving - he asking her to pretend to be his sister and so be taken by another man to wive; she suggesting surrogate motherhood heir adoption but feeling flaunted, losing her authority over Hagar. Like Abram before God, Sarai is no longer willing to remain silent before her lord and master:

And Sarai said to Abram: "The wrong done to me is your fault! I myself put my maid in your bosson now that she sees that she is pregnant, I am lowered in her esteem. The Lord decide between you and me!

Abram said to Sarai, "Your maid is in your hands. Deal with her as you think right."

Then Sarai treated her harshly and she ran away from her. (16:5-6).

The curious paradox is not Sarai's offer, nor her raging jealousy and vengeful treatment of her servant - which seem all too human - rather it is Abram's ambivalent behavior toward his unborn son and heir. He permitted Sarai to treat Hagar harshly, risking a miscarriage. He could have insisted that Hagar be properly cared for, or at least not tortured. Given his passionate desire for a son from his own loins, why did he display such indifference or impartial passivity toward Hagar and his unborn child?

One justification may be that in the rigid sexual segregation of pastoral home life, he may not have been aware of the extent of the abuse. But this does not explain the magnitude of his indifference. Without divine intervention, the child he had yearned for would be lost. The answer seems to lie in his ambivalence to fatherhood and patriarchy. His overearching desire for continuity were so important that they became a locus of intense ambivalence. He was threatened by what he most wanted; ironically, Abraham the ambivalent father, was the greatest danger to his own offspring, the son he wanted and feared.

The other pole of ambivalence concerns his checkered relation to his primary wife, Sarai. Here, when he is faced with a direct choice between preserving the marriage and ensuring children, he clearly opts for the marriage.

As argued above, Biblical biography gives precedence to ante-natal events, as crucial in determining a person's personality and destiny. Therefore, in the case of Ishmael and later for Isaac, much more narrative attention is given to events surrounding conception and birth, than say, early childhood - which would be crucial for any psychoanalytic biography.

The name "Ishmael" - "God hears" or "heeds" - has a double meaning. For Abram it is the fulfilment of the revelation (15:4-5) that God has heard his cry for a son of his own. For Hagar, as later for Ishmael, it symbolizes that God will pay heed to their suffering (21:17-21). The double meaning highlights another peculiar custom in Genesis of "double naming" in which mother and father separately confer the same name on their child. Many cultures specify whether father or mother (or uncle or priest) has the right to choose a child's name. In Genesis, we can see residue of competing maternal and paternal naming systems[51] - each naming the child for their own purposes. It is noteworthy that circumcision, for Abram-becoming-Abraham, as in contemporary Jewish practice, is the male, naming rite.

Ironically, Ishmael remained a common name in the Bible:[52] five other Ishmaels are listed (cf. II Kings 25:25; Jer. 40:41: Ezra 10:22: I Chronicles 8:38; 9:44; II Chronicles 19:11; 23:1) while the names Abraham, Isaac and Jacob never recur.

CHAPTER SIX:
ABRAM REBORN AS ABRAHAM

Ishmael's Childhood as a Stable Period in Abraham's Lifehistory

The interval between the birth of Ishmael and his circumcision is thirteen years, the age of Bar Mitzvah. This period constitutes a stable period of middle adulthood for Abram. No information is given for this period but there is no suggestion in the text that information has been suppressed. It is possible that no decisive event, either in the spiritual life of Abram, his relation with neighbors or in relation to his son occurred. There is, however, a clear indication (Gen. 17) that during this time Ishmael, who was growing from a child into a man, was inadequate. What was inadequate about him is never explicitly stated - but the revelation of chapter 17 made Ishmael retroactively an invalid heir. The commandment of circumcision ordained that a male child was to be circumcized on the eighth day Ishmael, on the other hand, was circumcized when he was thirteen, and moreover, his own father, Abram was uncircumcized at the time of his conception. Whatever Ishmael's personal qualities, he became, retroactively ritually unfit. Divine rejection of Ishmael meant that Abram's first attempt at fathering a "chosen son" was a failure.

The vision/revelation of the new covenants of circumcision-name change begin with the dramatic words: "I am El Shaddai: walk in My ways and be blameless ("tamim"). I will establish my covenant between me and you. I will make you exceedingly great" (17:1-2). The Hebrew verbal form for "walk" התהלך (hithaleickh") is the "hitpael", usually the reflexive construction, but here as in Mesopotamian languages means continuous action with the sense then of "Continue to walk in My ways." (cf. 5:22, 24; 6:9). The Hebrew תמים "tamim", translated as "blameless" or "devout", also means "whole or perfect" not in the sense of moral perfection, but rather in relation to God (von Rad 1976: 198). In the sense of Deut.18:13 "Be whole (tamim) with your God" cf. 20:5 in which "tam" is used as blameless, "without ulterior motives". Many ancient Hebrew sources (e.g. Targum Jonathan cf. Weinfeld 1982:119) regard "tamim" as "complete" in a physical sense: Cutting off the foreskin ('orla') removed the last imperfection.

Abraham's urge to "wholeness", in psychological terms, individuation, is contrasted with Noah's. Concerning Noah, it is written, "Noah was blameless ("tamim") in his age" (6:9). Noah's sense of being whole or blameless, is presented as an epithet, a fixed personality characteristic, not the result of an unfolding process as it is in "Abram-becoming-Abraham's" life history. Second, Noah's state is modified by the phrase which follows, "in his age" really in his "generation". Biblical History, we have argued, is often set against "generational" background and ancestral history, conceptualized as the 'sequence of generations' ("toledot") (cf. Levinson 1978:27-30; Ortega Y Gasset 1958). Noah was blameless, **but** only in his generation - his moral standing and individuation process great, only by comparison with the low standard; Abraham is urged to attain a sense of integration, of wholeness which could be **a model for all times**, in every generation, the prototype of "generative man".

Revitalizing Ritual of Middle Adulthood: The Meaning of Names

Names in the ancient Near East were symbols of continuity. In the Bible, to have one's name blotted out is the severest of punishment; to make one's name great, as the builders at Babel desired, is the greatest desire. Changing a name as part of initiation, especially in middle adulthood, means evoking, symbolizing a new identity, whose new destiny is revealed by his new name. "The name of a person determines his destiny" (Berachot 7b); changing one's name, like changing one's place, signifies a changed destiny.

A student of "the function and importance of the name in the psychology of the ancient Near East world" has noted that a name was not label or "convenient means of identification", but:

The name of a man was intimately involved in the very essence of his being and inextricably intertwined with his personality. Hence, giving a name is connected with creativity. An Egyptian theogonic myth tells how the first god Atum brought other gods into being by naming the parts of his body. In the Genesis cosmogony, God carefully gives a name to the first things He created, (except that in the scriptural demythologizing process the order has become reversed)...Conversely, anonymity is equivalent with non-being. Thus to "cut off the name" means to end existence, to annihilate, and in Egypt, with its death-centered religion, the way to bring an end to continued existence of a deceased person in the afterlife was by effacing his name from his tomb. The Torah legislates that when a man dies without issue his brother must take the widow as his wife and,

"The first son that she bears shall be accounted to the dead brother, that his name may not not be blotted out in Israel." (Deut. 25:6).

From all this it will be readily understood why the Bible invests name giving with such great importance and why a change of name is an event of major significance. Throughout the Near East the inauguration of a new era or a new state policy would frequently be marked by the assumption of a new name expressive of the change on the part of the King.
The very fact of a new name distinguishes and even effectuates, to an extent, the transformation of destiny...

(Sarna 1966:130-1).

In contemporary Israel, a society founded in defiance of traditional authority, continuity remains a dilemma. Among non-religious Jews, children are no longer named for relatives as was done traditionally. Such neologisitc naming, making up new names, or using "new" names from Bible or elsewhere, indicates that native-born Israelis were and are to have a destiny different from their parents or grandparents. In a recent survey of naming practices (Abramovitch & Bilu 1985), we found that:

"There was a virtual absence of the most common traditional Jewish forenames - such as Miriam, Rachel, Solomon or David. Among all 387 names, stalwarts of Jewish identity such as "Moshe" or "Hayyim" occurred only once. It will be noticed that the majority of the most common names cited above are short and neologistic. Some are derived from nature, such as Daphna (laurel tree), Tal (dew), or Oren (pine-tree), while others are cognates of the Hebrew word for "light" or "joy" - such as Lior (a light unto me) or Roni (my joy). Names derived from the Bible are often those of peripheral personalities, such as Yael, Asaph or Michal; they are not those of the familiar heroes of the Old Testament - Abraham, Isaac or Jacob. Biblical names such as Omri and Hagar were not traditionally given to Jewish children, since Omri was a great but an immoral king (I Kings 16:16-26), while Hagar was Sarai's maid whom she gave to Abram so that she might bear him children and she bore him Ishmael, who would have "every man's hand against him" (Genesis 16:1-12).

"Kibbutz parents said that they chose a scriptural name not because of its Biblical connotations but merely because they liked the sound of it. Such a general attitude about naming children represents a break with the former inter-generational pattern, and to that extent may reflect an underlying desire on the part of younger Israelis to distance themselves from the traditional value systems of their often immigrant parents. The new names have no moral or religious connotations; they are more like labels which bear no relationship to any facet of the personality" (Abramovitch & Bilu 1985:15).

For Abram to become Abraham, the name change is a marker event of recognition that a transformation has taken place, a transformation of identity and destiny.

This change of name communicates to others, as much to himself, his new spiritual and psychological status.

From "Av-ram" to "Av-raham"

The word play, so beloved in Hebrew Bible, of the name change indicates a changed relation to paternity. Although the Text does not provide an etymology for Abram, in Hebrew it can be easily broken down into two linguistic components, אב "av", (father) and רם "ram" (high, exalted, supreme, raised up). The meaning may be "(my) father is supreme". The name "abram" (or its cognate Abi-Ram) has not been encountered in ancient documents (De Vaux 1978), although names such as Abam-rama, Aba-rama or Abam-ram have. The sister of Sanncherib's favorite wife was called Abu(AD)-rami, which in Akkadian means "loves the father", but which according to De Vaux "comes from the root r'm, 'to love', which does not exist in western Semitic" (De Vaux 1978:197). Whatever the actual meaning of "av-ram" it suggests an exalted relation to Father. Such a relation, which we argue may have played an early role in the development of Abram's God-image in which feelings toward his father became transferred to the voice which called him away from father. Now, "Abram, son of Terah", disappears and in his place is reborn a new "Avraham" son of El Shaddai. The name change, as we noted above (cf Rendsburg 1986) divides the narratives about Abram/Abraham in half; in the first five chapters of his life story he is "Abram", afterward he is known as "Abraham". The new name, new destiny, new paternity and as we shall discuss a radically new relation with his Divine Father all make the naming-circumcision ritual pivotal.

The change of the name from "av-ram" to "av-raham" symbolizes changed relations to "father". The new name "av-raham" אברהם shifts the focus from Abraham's father, to Abraham's own role as "father", indeed a "Great Father", the "Father of Many". The neologism indicates and consolidates his new identity as a "Father" progenitor in his own right; not based on his relation to his father. The name change is a middle adulthood rite of passage (circa age 50) of re-creation and renewal which resolves his first crisis of generativity.

The new name is given a literary contrast in the story (20:1-18) which follows. The name of the King of Gerar upon whom the "wife/sister" act is played, is אבימלך "avi-melech", which in Hebrew means, "my father the King". Indeed the same name turns up in the a second fooling of the King of Gerar (26:6-16), although it is not clear whether it is the same king[53] or his lineal descendant, son or grandson, who keep the same dynastic name (cf. Henry I, II, III etc.). The root "av", "father" is found in both names and, as Rendsburg has shown, common roots and motif words link adjoining sections in the Abraham narrative. The name "avimelech", "my father, the King" is like "avram", a name which honors the father, indicating implicitly an inferior position of the son.

The King's name "my father the king" is a name which indicates what sociologists call "ascribed status". In this case, Avimelech becomes king because his father was king, not necessarily because of any achievement of his own. "Achieved status", in contrast, is the status one obtains by personal effort. Conquering a land and declaring one's self king is an example of achieved status. The contrasting tension between achieved and ascribed status is very much apropos the move from Avram to Avraham, from Isaac to Ishmael, from Elon Moreh to Beersheba. Until his circumcision-name change ritual of self creation, he was, in name at least, his father's son. The revitalizing ritual, naming, describes the move from an ascribed status as a "son" to an achieved status as a "father", from his father's son into his sons' father.

In contemporary Palestinian society, as well as many others which practice naming a father after the son, a parent is called by the name of his child; thus a man is known not by his given name, but as "father of Musa" (**abu musa**) or "mother of Musa" (**umm musa**). If a man or woman have no children (or no sons), then one might honor them by calling them by the name they would have, if they had children. Becoming a parent is thus an achieved status, and as in Genesis, it is the most important or rather most basic achieved status, an event which "marks" a man's life as irrevocably changed. (Muhawi and Kanaana 1989).

The acquisition of a new name indicating paternity formulates a biological mode of symbolic immortality: "I am changed, because my children and their children after them will carry on my name, identity, values etc" (cf. 18:19). The circumcision ritual, however, is designed to mark a transition to spiritual paternity, from father of a single son to Father of many. Here, I believe, is a way to understand the rejection of Ishmael as the first promised child. The "firstborn", Ishmael, derived his status, from being Abraham's son i.e. his status was ascribed not achieved. But for Ishmael to be a spiritual "son" or disciple of Abraham, he must likewise move from his ascribed biological status to an achieved status as spiritual son of the prophet. The gap in the lifehistory between chapter 16 and 17, i.e. from Ishmael's birth to his circumcision hints at the failure of Ishmael to achieve his expected promised status as a spiritual heir. Ishmael, as his name indicates, will also be "heard" by God, but his destiny is as an "other"; rejected, exiled, he will be forced to go his own way, and thereby achieve an independent identity of his own.[54]

Changing a name thus represents a change in social status, as when a woman changes her "family" name from that of her father to that of her husband; or, as for Ishmael as part of a puberty rite. As such name change also functions to symbolize an inner change, a culmination of an intiation process. It is as if the new name shows, as much to one's self as to all others that: "I am not the person I used to be; I am different; I have changed." The social person one used to be, with all the duties, obligations and feelings, is "dead" and gone; a new person is "reborn" in his place. In a "born again" identity, one is no longer responsible to the feelings and the duties associated with the "old name" and old identity.

Such a logic of "death and rebirth" permeate all rites of initiation: the old self identity dies and a new one is reborn in its place. In the context of the circumcision-naming ritual, Ishmael is reborn as a man, his boyhood self dies; and he is brought under the omnipresent paternity of the Divine Heavenly Father. For Abraham such a ritual is one that may be characterized not as "twice born" but "thrice born" (Turner 1978). He had been "reborn" as Abu-Ishmael, the father of Ishmael; now at 99 he is about to become "thrice born": Hindu culture uses the metaphor of "twice born" to describe rebirth in spiritual life of a Brahmin; likewise an anthropologist may undergo a series of symbolic rebirths:

> *The first birth is our natal origin in a particular culture. The second is our move from this familiar to a far away place to do field work there...The third birth occurs when we have become become comfortable within the other culture - and found the clue to grasping many like it - and turn our gaze again toward our native land. We find that the familiar has become exoticized; we see it with new eyes. What we took for granted now has the power to stir our scientific imaginations..."Thrice born" anthropologists are perhaps in the best position to become the "reflexivity"of a culture".*

(Turner in Myerhoff 1978:xiii-xiv).

I am not suggesting, of course that Abraham was an anthropologist, except insofar that any migrant or refugee performs the similar tasks of trying to understand the rules for interaction of his "adopted" culture in terms of his "native" one. Abraham, like a "senior" ethnographer, deciphered the rules not of a single foreign realm, but of at least five cultures: southern Mesopotamia, northern Mesopotamia/Kurdistan; Egypt, Judean Hill country (Hebron, etc.); Negev (Beersheva; Gerar). To this extent Abram, the first Hebrew, is also the archetypal model of the "wandering Jew".

The name change did not indicate a total rejection of the past, but rather the initiation of a new identity and destiny. Such name changes are common in the lives of spiritual revolutionaries and are external signs of some inner transformation. After his dramatic conversion on the road to Damascus, Saul the Hebrew becomes Paul, the follower of Christ. After his enlightenment Prince Siddharta is known as Gautama the Buddha. Most recently, Communist leaders of spiritual-political movements likewise practiced neonymy, such as the lawyer Vladimir Ulyanov who became Nicolai Lenin, Marxist Revolutionary. Many religious or political organizations require new members to foresake their old names and acquire new ones.

The Meanings of Circumcision as a "Marker Event"

The covenantal circumcision of Abraham and his household appeared to follow an Egyptian pattern of ritual group circumcision (Pritchard 1967), in which hundreds of men of a certain age or status were circumcised **en masse**. Group circumcision of that sort was intended to bond its participants into a blood brotherhood; Abraham's rite presumably was intended to create such a brother-hood among all the male members of his clan, uniting them with Abraham under the authority and protection of YHWH. Moreover it sanctified the sexuality of members of his camp. At other times in Egypt circumcision was restricted to the priestly class, thereby adding a further dimension and exclusivity to the act. But in Egypt it was also known as a medical procedure to relieve infections or swellings under the foreskin, (Penfeld 1935) from which Abram may have suffered.

Abram's circumcision of himself was an act of self-creation. He initiated the promised spiritual and familial patriarchy in himself - literally in his own flesh. In circumcising his entire household, he affirmed his authority and patriarchy over them and Ishmael in particular. By imposing his covenant upon them Abraham became their spiritual father. Yet nothing further was heard of the brotherhood in Genesis and their inconsequential disintegration must count as another one of Abraham's failures.

Note that a life cycle approach to circumcision[55] asserts that such a ritual has different meanings at different ages. e.g. For Abraham it is an act of self-creation and altered relation to generativity and sexuality, increasing the importance of the penis (and perhaps a necessary surgical procedure); for Ishmael it is a puberty rite of male initiation, involving both submitting to his father's (and Father's) will but also assisting him in the difficult transition from boyhood to manhood by this marker event, which shuts tight the regressive door back to childhood and infantile sexuality; for Isaac it is a mark of (future) separation from mother and marking his penis with the sign of God.

For all three it has the effect of sanctifying what would otherwise be "tainted" viz. sexuality. For Abraham it clearly serves to rejuvenate his sexual performance; for Ishmael it marks his entry into adult sexuality, the possibility of fatherhood; for Isaac it is an unconscious acceptance of sexuality as something "divine". For all three then it is a symbol of separation and rebirth.

Circumcision, for an adolescent like Ishmael is a masculine ordeal. He must be "man enough" to bear the pain and, if successful, will emerge with a new respect for himself. For an infant like Isaac, circumcision is perhaps no less an ordeal but one which, for the baby, consists of senseless pain.

The implications for spiritual development seem clear. A man's (but not a woman's) relation with the God of Abraham begin unconsciously, in a senseless pain which only gradually regains significance as a mark in the tribal-spiritual blood brotherhood. It also suggests that, in general, relationships with the Divinity are initiated by senseless pain, suffering, violence which only subsequently may have meaning as part of some pre-ordained plan. Finally, if "circumcision is the symbolic substitute of castration" (Freud 1939:192), then infant circumcision is a particularly successful displacement of the paternal urge to castrate his sons, since it is ritually done (and approved), when the son has no ability to resist, nor the father any cause (yet) for anger.

But beyond being an element of initiating ritual, Abraham's use of circumcision had spiritual and psychological implications. All male children born under Abraham's patriarchy are to be circumcised eight days after birth. This innovation changed the dynamics of the ordeal from initiation into an adult group to an infant initiation into an ageless life of the spirit. In this way the ritual act was made the decision of the father of the child, who inducted the boy by blood rite into the covenant with El Shaddai. The boy had no part in the decision and grew to maturity thus marked with the symbol of his blood brotherhood with all Hebrews. The ritual appropriately was practiced upon the very instrument of procreation and continuity, sanctifying sexuality with a formal sign of YHWH's approval.

A descendant of Abraham cannot choose to be a "Hebrew" but can exercise a real choice only on behalf of his sons. If he does not circumcise them, he cuts them off not only from himself but also from his own spiritual community.

Even though the practice of circumcision lapsed during Hebrew's sojourn in Egypt and the desert (cf. Moses' sons' circumcision (Ex.4:24-6) and Joshua's mass circumcision (Josh. 5:2-5), the rite still forms a direct link to Abraham and his God and precedes all Mosaic Law and Ritual. It still remains the prime identifier of the Hebrew. In creating a new identity for himself, Abraham succecded in devising a lasting identity for all his spiritual-sons.

The third part of the covenant provided the specific details of Abraham's great lineage. He would have a son with Sarah and the covenant would be maintained through that son and his offspring. When Abraham heard this, he was incredulous. He laughed in his heart. (Hebrew: יצחק "Yitzchak") He was almost a hundred years old and his wife was nearly ninety. But the Lord affirmed that the son would be born in one year's time and that he would be called Yitschak, i.e., Isaac.

During this discussion Abraham suddenly raised the possiblity that the Lord may kill Ishmael, in giving him Yitschak.[56] This was the second manifestation of Abraham's ambivalence - even of his latent murderous desires - toward Ishmael. His fears here are reminiscent of his earlier expressions of anxiety in Genesis 15 and of his practice of confiding the worst. But it also pointed ahead to Ishmael's expulsion and close brush with death, and even more decisively to the time when Abraham again becomes convinced that YHWH desires the death of his "son of his own laughter", Isaac. If Ishmael, however, was a "failure" for Abraham, then he might well harbor murderous wishes toward him and so projecting onto God his own unacceptable impulse.

A short time, three days (based on comparison with Genesis 34:25), the Lord, in the guise of three travellers, appears to Abraham. In keeping with nomadic traditions of hospitality, Abraham graciously fed and provided for the strangers. In addition to the etiquette of nomadic hospitality Abraham had another reason for welcoming the strangers: It gave him his first recorded opportunity to affirm and demonstrate his new name. Abraham, with his new name and confidence, dominated his wife - he ordered her to bake bread for his guests and later rebuked her for not believing that she would bear a son, though he himself had inwardly laughed at the same news.

During the "visit" the Lord repeated his prophecy that Sarah would have a son and Sarah, eavesdropping, laughed at the thought. When YHWH challenged her concerning her disbelief over her promised pregnancy, she denied her laughter; but Abraham triumphed over her by asserting with divine witness that she had, as in fact he had, laughed. This triumph - and the imposition of her new name - indicated the reassertion of his authority over the barren Sarah. Without children, Sarah still had no permanent status, as Genesis 20 proved. She was still more a sister than a wife. But once she bore her son, Abraham never again subjugated her. She grew in strength until she achieved her own triumph over Abraham in having Hagar and Ishmael permanantly expelled and disinherited, giving her, literally, the "last laugh".

In becoming Abraham, Abram established a new form of symbolic continuity for all his progeny: each son must accept Abraham as father, generation after generation, to sustain the Hebrew tradition and receive its benefits. Abraham, however, made the choice for all his progeny. They participate or are "cut off". In Erikson's apt phrase, Abraham solved for all his sons what he could not solve for himself alone, a lasting fatherhood of sons-becoming-fathers in the presence of a Heavenly Father.

Divine Monologue, Human Dialogue

After the standoff between husband and wife as to who laughed, the Hebrew Text becomes ambiguous and difficult to visualize. Chapter 18 began with the phrase: "The Lord appeared to him by the terebinths of Mamre;" (18:1) and then Abraham looking up to see three men standing near him. Later, after the men have gone onto Sodom, the Text continues, "Abraham remained standing before the Lord. Abraham came forward and said, "Will you sweep away the innocent along with the guilty?" (18:22-3).

Morever, when Abraham greets the three men, he calls them in Hebrew אדני "adonai", which J.P.S. translates as "my lords" but adds in a footnote or "My Lord". Does the opening verse (18:1) refer to the three visitors one of whom is "The Lord"? Or does the phrase, "The Lord appeared to him..." function as a chapter heading covering the events of the entire chapters, as in the opening phrase of the "akeda", "God put Abraham to the test" (22:1), which refers to all the subsequent events in the rest of the chapter. Likewise, in 18:22 when Abraham is standing before the Lord and responding to what he has heard, is the Lord one of the three men who appeared so mysteriously or is the Lord some unseen but heard Presence as He was for the child Samuel, who responds "heneni" "Here I am", as Abraham does twice during the akeda.

What can be said with certainty is that the ambiguity is in the Text itself. And why? I would spectulate that the lack of clarity may possibly reflect changing notions in the Hebrew "God-image" as to whether the Lord might appear in human form. The ambiguity persists in the extraordinary soliloquy (18:17-19), surely one of the remarkable in all Scripture. The narrative flow until this point has been of one description from the point of view of an external observer, interspersed with dialogue. It is true that concerning Sarah it is written, "And Sarah laughed to herself, saying, "Now that I am withered, am I to have enjoyment - with my husband so old?" (but the Lord knows that she has secretly laughed and challenges her "Is anything too wondrous for the Lord?" (18:14).) Likewise, in the following passage v. 17-19 we appear to enter into the inner thoughts of "the character of the Lord", overhearing Him convince Himself to do something He is not entirely sure about - as if this revelation not to "hide from Abraham what I am about to do" (19:16) is the real test for the Lord. Whatever one may think about narrative theology of divine doubts, it is clear from the Text that the character of the Lord feels Himself to have mutual obligations with Abraham and His descendants:

Shall I hide from Abraham what I am about to do, since Abraham is to become a great and populous nation and all the nations of the earth are to bless

themselves by him? For I have singled him out, that he may instruct his
children and his posterity to keep the way of the Lord by doing what is right
and just, in order that the Lord may bring about for Abraham what He has
promised him (18:17-19).

Just as I suggested that Abraham's god-image develops and matures, so too, the "character of the Lord" within Genesis appear to change and develop. I use the term "god-image" to differentiate it from "God" or "the Lord" and focus on how the Divine appears in the Text without speculating as to what He really may be.

A full discussion of the changing "god-image" within the Bible is well beyond the scope of the present work, but I will suggest a few issues which seem relevant to our concerns. "In the beginning", God creates order out of disorder; He has speech and His very words are creative. "God said, "Let there be light"; and there was light." (1:3) He is able to evaluate, to separate and to name (1:4), qualities He will pass onto his human creations. Once created, his creations like the biosphere, are no longer dependent upon Him, but have a momentum of their own, in a natural cycle.

The key phrase in the creation of humanity, "Let us make man in our image, after our likeness" (1:26) suggests that there is some similarity between man and God. Although the exact nature of the likeness is never stated explicitly, it is clear that man, at first, is created without moral knowledge, which is an attribute of the Creator. Once Adam and his wife eat of the fruit of the tree of knowledge of good and bad, it is only immortality which separates them from God. (3:22).

The anxiety of the character of God at this juncture appears that if the couple are left in the Garden, then even this distinction may be taken away: "... What if he should stretch out his hand and take also from the tree of life and eat, and live forever" (3:22) as if, even eternal life was once within man's grasp, but no more. For all His threats of dire punishment to Adam and to Cain, his punishments are mediated by compassion - not death as promised but banishment; and for Cain even a protective sign. The character of God appears as a stern but caring Father.

In relation to his "creations", the character of God is compassionate. He worries about their welfare ("It is not good for man to be alone." 2:18), hands over to humankind His original "naming function" (2:19), tries to console a wayward "grandson" (4:6-7) but challenges and curses disobedience and wrongdoing in Eve, Adam and Cain. The character of God does not appear in Chapters 4:17-5:32 but reappears dramatically in chapter 6:3 "My breath shall not abide in man forever, since he too is flesh; Let the days allowed him be 120 years", further setting humankind apart from Himself (possibly reflected in an ironic reference to "divine beings", which theology escatology aside, probably refers to nobles who considered themselves divine and deny the fundamental difference between men and God.)

The most important phrase, for our purposes, is His view of human wickedness: *"The Lord saw how great was man's wickedness on earth and how every plan devised by his mind was nothing but evil all the time. And the Lord regretted that He had made man on earth and His heart was saddened (6:5-6).*

The character of the Lord, unlike the "god of the Philosophers", is not all-knowing but suffers from regret. Like an artist, critically evaluating his work, the character of the Lord sees the clear signs of an artistic failure and impulsively wishes to blot out the evidence of his own failure. The shift from a total rejection of humankind as "nothing but evil" reflects an ability to maintain a personal individualized relationship, but not with humanity as a whole, but with a specific individual and his family. Such a shift prefigures His relationship with Abraham when He says, "For I have singled him out..." (18:19).

Saving Noah not only reinitiates a personalized relation between a specific person and the Lord, but resembles the link between creativity and destructiveness in the creative artist who is able to save one "grace-ful" element in the flawed masterpieced so as to start anew. The character of God, however, seems almost to gain insight into His own impulsivity (a characteristic which Moses must deal with repeatedly) and seeks to limit His own destructive impulsivity - as if to echo Abraham's opening line that at Sodom as in the Flood, innocent and guilty were swept away together. Like many contemporary Holocaust survivors, God the Surviver says, "Never again!" and binds himself in mutual obligation with the descendants of Noah. But his relationship is not with humanity as a whole but with a single individual and his descendants who will represent Him to the rest of humankind.

The story of the tower of Babel (presumably a Biblical comment on Mesopotamina Temple Religion, with its towering ziggurats) shows a less impulsivity. The Text does not make it clear what is the wrongdoing of the Tower Builders. One might assume, like in the Garden, the threat is that humankind will supplant God or even with an Oedipal flourish displace Him as God the Father. At Babel, the character of God is not impulsive. He investigates, foresees the problem before it comes to a head and creates an elegant strategy to dissipate the potential threat by "pseudospeciation" via language diversity, fragmenting the natural unity within the family of man into autonomous linguistic (and ethnic) units. Note that within the Biblical cosmogy, language is basic and preceeds creation. Unlike many other religions, there is no "myth of the creation of speech"; rather what needs to be explained is linguistic diversity, which again may be viewed as a subtle form of banishment, as in words of the Text, "the Lord scattered them over the face of the earth" (11:9).

From the point of view of His creatures, The Lord as Creator, Eternal, Moral

Authority acts like stern but caring Father who conquers his impulsive nature. Yet, such a view suggests that within the hearts of biblical men, there is a persistent anxiety that God as Father might abandon or annihilate them.

It is against such divine separation anxiety that the development of Abraham's Covenant may be understood.

CHAPTER SEVEN:
CRISES OF GROWTH

"First Hebrew Prophet"

The major spiritual advance of this period of Abraham's life was the development of a new relationship with his God. Some of his experiences of the presence of YHWH had been full of "fear and trembling". In his later years, while he had occasionally mustered enough nerve to complain, or had felt incredulous toward YHWH's pronouncements, he ultimately always followed YHWH' s orders without question.

However, when YHWH announced the impending destruction of Sodom, Abraham, out of his new-found sense of intimacy and communion with YHWH, found the courage to challenge his Lord. While mindful of his own inconsequence as "a man of dust and ashes", Abraham rose stalwartly to the defense of his neighbors - however morally corrupt - in terms of what he saw to be universal principles of justice. To realize the profound spiritual growth represented by Abraham's fearless challenge to YHWH's ultimate authority, we can compare his staunch advocacy of justice here with his own earlier passiveness and particularly with Cain's whimpering protest (4:13-14) and Noah's silence (7:5) in the face of their own overwhelming encounters with death.

The scope of Abraham's new relationship with YHWH is indicated by the fact that his spirited defense of the men of Sodom is no longer an exercise in tribal particularism as in his rescue of Lot. Quite fittingly, Abraham's first exercise in spiritual patriarchy makes the relation between YHWH and all "men of dust and ashes" a relation between moral equals. Men must survive in order for YHWH to exist as a guiding moral force in the world. Without mankind's recognition, without men to carry out his way, YHWH must himself cease to survive among men. It was the achievement of this understanding of equality that permanently rid Abraham of his fear and trembling.

In arguing humankind's case to God, Abraham defines the role of "Hebrew Prophet" as one who is not only God's messanger on earth but humankind's advocate "in heaven". Later in this tumultous year, when he prays successfully for the woman of Gerar, he is called the "prophet", the first use of the term ("navi") in Scripture so that Abraham is rightly not only the First Father but also the Founding Prophet. (cf Exodus 7:1).

The new morality for which Abraham so forcefully argued arose from his own double commitment to justice. His first commitment was to the belief that there is justice in the world. This belief followed from his personal conviction that there is a universal creator spirit in the world who embodies all that is "just and right." The Mesopotamians, in contrast, who did not share such a universal vision of the divine spirit, were committed to the worship of divinities who had created man for their own service and pleasure. Scholars (e.g. Speiser, 1964) and students of ancient Mesopotamia have remarked that the cosmos of the great civilization of the land between the rivers lacked an ethical base. Man was not created to fulfill a plan of creation or divine morality, but "to serve the gods so that their life would be easy", according to **Enuma Elish**, their epic of creation. It was such an amoral conception of the world which Abram rejects in his poignant plea: "Shall the judge of the world not act justly?" (18:25)

In the literature of the Ancient Near East there is a revealing contrast to Genesis 18:25. The **Lament over the Destruction of Ur**, (Kramer 1940), Abraham's native city, contains a passage which stands in opposition to Abraham's eloquent pleas. In that document the patron god of Ur appealed the ongoing desolation of his city and shrine to his father, one of the chief gods. He was told that "the decree had come down" from the divine council and could not be changed; nor ought one to expect kingship to remain in one city forever. The destruction of the city therefore remained incomprehensible, carried out at the whim of the gods. We see that Abraham argued against such a view. His God had called mankind - and himself specifically - into being to serve a specific moral purpose. To be a universal God, Abraham's God must be subject to ethical constraints which are, on the whole, available to human awareness. Abraham could "know" God by embodying this moral avocation in his own life and teaching. To deny the prevailing force of justice and goodness in the world was therefore tantamount to denying the existence of Abraham's universal God. If the existence of YHWH or his moral principle was questionable, then the whole basis of Abraham's mission, to be a blessing to all the nations, would be negated. The overthrow of Sodom (like the future overthrow of the kingdoms of Israel and Judah, 2 Kings 17:7-23 or the military defeats of Joshua 7:1-26) was not therefore the result of power, necessity or chance, but the natural "karmic" result of moral and social decay.

The threat to the moral order contained in the impending disaster at Sodom also has its implications for Abraham's personal commitment to justice. If the innocent and the guilty were to be treated alike, then what might save Abraham or his descendants from a similar fate? If the just Sodomites could be killed without reason, then why not Abraham and his seed? The continuity of Abraham's mission and the universality of his blessing depended on the priviledged survival of his line. This survival in turn was a function of their morally superior and divinely inspired life style. But if innocent and guilty alike might be destroyed, then even a morally superior life style would be no guarantee of continuity (15:16). He and his seed might all be wiped off the face of the earth, overnight, like the inhabitants of the cities of the plain.

Abraham's argument with YHWH therefore generated a moral order which must be followed not only by Abraham and his descendants but also by YHWH as well: the Judge of all men must Himself be just! Henceforth YHWH could not act as he pleased, for he was constrained by the mutuality of the covenant. This position led to the evolution of the new concept of the "saving grace of the just". In contrast to the harsh justice of his time, Abraham demonstrated that for the sake of the covenant YHWH must err on the side of compassion, must always be ready to temper the law with mercy, to permit a multitude of wicked to survive lest even a few just men - Abraham and YHWH agree on 10 as the minimum moral community - should suffer. His spirited defense of the Sodomites contrasted with his earlier concern for himself and his kin. His previous saving of Sodom was motivated by a strong sense of family honor: the need to rescue Lot. Now he pleaded for the city despite his personal dislike of the townsfolk, and in spite of Lot's presence in the city. Significantly, Abraham never mentioned Lot in the debate but argued along universal humanitarian lines, thereby attaining universal status as a defender of mankind.

The holocaust at Sodom engendered another equally important aspect of Abraham's spiritual growth: it made graphically clear that Abraham and entourage are the chosen of the Lord, selected "to keep the way of the Lord, to do what is just and right."... The rewards of keeping the Lord's way were explicitly portrayed in Abraham's new relation with the Lord, in the great ethical and spiritual advances he made, second to the covenant YHWH sealed with him on behalf of mankind. The penalties for not keeping the Lord's way were made clear in the story of the Flood, the story of Babel, the holocaust at Sodom and, at a more personal level, in the story of Lot.

"Four Reactions To Trauma: Sodom and Post-Traumatic Stress"

The events surrounding the destruction of the cities of the Plain, described in the latter half of Ch. 18:16-33 and Ch. 19, contrast the more distant reaction of Abraham to those more intensively affected by this catastrophe. Taken together these responses present a panorama of four prototypical reactions to trauma, from the frozen stasis of Lot's wife to the survivor mission of the newly circumcized Patriarch.

The first paradigmatic response to the threat of imminent disaster is **denial**. This is the response of Lot's sons-in-law who when informed by Lot of the disaster "thought he was joking" (Gen. 19:14).

A student of collective behavior during disasters has witten:

Many people tend to deny or disbelieve information that danger is near at hand. They seize on any vagueness ambiguity, or incompatibility in the warning message enabling them to interpret the situation optimistically...often they continue to interpret signs of danger as signs of familiar, normal events until it is too late to take effective action precautions.

(Fritz 1961:665)

Ordinarily, such "holocausts" are unbelievable. (Abramovitch 1986). In contrast, individuals who have had some prior experience with disaster of traumatic proprtions do tend to heed warnings, to respond effectively during the trauma and to be less vulnerable to the lasting negative effects.

Traumatic events, such as natural disasters, modern warfare, concentration camps or traffic accidents often leave victims permanently scarred. Although they emerge physically intact, they may be emotionally consumed by the event, unable to resume their previous identity and existence. Instead, their identity as a survivor overtakes them. They become first and foremost (and often exclusively) survivors, frozen emotionally within the psychological confines of their catastrophe, unable to get clear. Like one blinded by the unexpected flash of a lightbulb, the energies of the survivor are absorbed by the unexpected intensity of the event. In extreme cases, victims are said to be suffering from a new and seemingly ubiquitous psychiatric diagnosis, post-traumatic stress disorder or PTSD, for short. "The characteristic symptoms involve re-experiencing the traumatic event, numbing of responsiveness to or involvement with external world ..." (DSM III). Sufferers of PTSD often relive the trauma, for instance in recurrent nightmares which rerun the traumatic episode in such excruciating intensity that they often awake screaming. At the same time, victims exhibit a diminished or constricted responsiveness that has been referred to as "psychic numbing" or "emotional anesthesia", which is felt to be a distinct change from the pre-traumatic condition. He or she is thus unable to become interested or enjoy previously satisfying activities. He feels detached or estranged from others and indeed almost incapable of feeling emotions of any type, especially the bonding emotions such as intimacy, tenderness or sexuality.

The reaction of Lot's wife is a typical PTSD reaction of a person who may physically escape but does not really survive emotionally. Looking back, against the (mental health) advice of the messengers, she is turned into a pillar of salt. For our metaphorical purposes, Lot's wife (one in a long series of nameless Biblical women) is frozen in the process of looking back at the trauma scene. Although we are not explicitly told in the Biblical text, it seems reasonable to suppose that she was a native of Sodom and therefore experienced a greater sense of violation and loss than the newcomer Lot. In a sense Lot has lost a world (he has seen others; Ur, Haran, Egypt) but for his wife, she has lost her world, which was the world. Like sufferers of PTSD, she is unable to feel anything except the trauma. The intensity of the event overwhelms her. She is unable to get clear and flee with her family to start a new life. Like other victims of PTSD she spends her life "looking back" without the possibility of "looking forward". This terrible past takes the place and blots out the future. For readers of the Bible who knew of the strange geological formations in the barren landscape near the Dead Sea, these salt pillars remained a lasting memorial, a physical reminder of the awesome power of divine destruction and retribution.

If Lot's wife personifies the acute, frozen numbing response, then her husband Lot exemplifies a more insidious but chronic variant of PTSD. Lot is weak, pathetic, victimized. He takes to drink presumably in an attempt to escape dealing with the traumatic loss, to become numb. The moral ambigulty of his responses clearly evokes the post-traumatic response of an earlier survivor of a total disaster, Noah, after the flood.

Noah introduces alcohol into the human society. He becomes, while drunk, the passive victim of incest. The story of Noah is given in Gen. 9:20-26:

Noah, the tiller of the soil, was the first to plant a vineyard. He drank of the wine and became drunk, and he uncovered himself within his tent. Ham, the father of Canaan, saw his father's nakedness and told his two brothers outside. But Shem and Japeth took a cloth, placed it against both their backs and walking backwards, they covered their father's nakedness. When Noah woke

up from his wine and learned what his youngest son had done to him, he said:
"Cursed be Canaan;
The lowest of slaves
Shall he be to his brothers."

and he said,

"Blessed be the Lord,
The God of Shem
Let Canaan be a slave to them.

"May God enlarge Japeth
And let him dwell in the tents of Shem;
And let Canaan be a slave to them."

The Hebrew phrase, "uncover his father's nakedness" refers to improper sexual activity and in other contexts seems to refer to sexual intercourse not merely exposed genitals. (cf. Lev. 18:6f.) Indeed David Bakan has argued ("The Gender of Noah" in "And They Took Themselves Wives: The Emergence of Patriarchy in Western Civilization", Harper & Row 1979 pp. 77-82) due to pecularities of the text, such as gender changes (e.g. "her" tent instead of the expected "his" tent) that the Noah figure was changed from a male to a female. In that case, the situation would even more directly parallel Lot's daughters, with Canaan, Ham's son the presumptive incestuous offspring of their illicit union.

Many scholars have pointed out that the blend of geneology ("toledot") and improper sexual practices and incestuous unions and Canaan, Moab, and Ammon provide a cognitive map of the degree of relatedness and taintedness. Edmund Leach, in his well known essay "Genesis as Myth", puts it "that a rank order is established which places the tribal neighbors of the Israelites in varying degrees of inferior status depending upon the nature of the defect in their original ancestry as compared with the pure descent of Jacob (Israel)" (Leach 1967:21). Canaan is of a lower status and moral standing than Ammon and Moab.[58]

Lot's reaction, his alcoholism, the breakdown of norms and taboos began even before the disaster, when he offered his daughters to be raped instead of his messenger-guests. (Cf. the parallel story in Judges 19). This offer involving sexual license attains an ironic twist when his nakedness is uncovered. The Sodomites' depravity, their desire for homosexual gang rape (an image of ultimate sexual horror) is connnected with an implcit condemnation of urban life and values, going back to Cain, who founded the first city for his son. In contrast, the Biblical ideal is that of the free wandering pastoral life, exemplified by Abraham, Jacob, Moses and the young David, who live with geographical insecurity but within the presence of God. Disasters occasionally cause "breakdown of moral code", although this is not the general case. In the contrast between Lot and his daughters, we see two modes in which such a breakdown may occur. For Lot, incest is unconscious, out of his control. He is a passive, unknowing, victim and the violation of this basic taboo is part of his numbing response. Lot's daughters, on the other hand, knowingly and willingly violate the most basic taboo of family life, as part of their survivor mission, to assure the biological continuity of the species (or their family) : "...let us lie with him that we may maintain life through our father" (Gen. 19:32).

In contemporary Western society the most common form of incest is father-daughter intercourse. Such incest, even when it is not overt rape, usually carries with it an implicit threat on the part of the father of violence, coercion, threat of reprisal or "forced silence" toward his child victim. (Butler 1979; Lister 1982; Herman & Hirschman 1982). Lot's daughters do not conform to this pattern, since they initiate the violation of social taboo, not for sexual pleasure or power, but for the continuity of life.

Moreover, this pair of sisters operates in sharp contrast to other sister[59] (Rachal-Leah) or co-wives (Sarah-Hagar) i.e. without sexual competition or reproductive envy. In the case of Lot's daughers, the "proper order" of elder before younger is followed, indeed the elder urges the younger to follow her example. (Ideologically in terms of geneology as a congitive map of ethnic relatedness by folk etymology, Moab is conceived as dominant i.e. senior, elder to Bene-Ammon.) If the story has psychosexual import, it does not seem to contain a hint of Electra Complex, except perhaps the hidden fantasy to have a child with one's father but rather the unconscious sexual desire of a father toward his daughters ("He did not know when she lay down or when she rose" v. 33).

The cooperation of these sisters may also reflect their post-disaster state, since "widespread sharing of danger loss and deprivation produces an intimate primary group solidarity among survivors which overcomes social isolation and provides a channel for intimate communication and expression and a major source of physical and emotional support and reassurance" (Fritz 1961:689).

If as psychoanalysts may argue the story contains the repressed wish on the part of daughters to have a magical child with their father, then it all the more points to the unconscious sexual desire of fathers toward their nubile daughters ("he did not know when she lay down nor when she rose" 19:33), which as recent surveys reveal is much more the destructive norm. (cf. Dworkin 1987:229 "Perhaps incestuous rape is becoming a central paradigm for intercourse in our time...")

What is striking in the narrative style of Gen. 19 is how the figures of Lot's daughters (and later Hagar, Ishmael and even Esau) are portrayed in detail and with sympathy, despite the tainted descent of their descendants. The sympathy and narrative focus fits with the universalistic mood of Genesis 18, which asserts the human character of wrongdoers or neighboring enemies. Such universal humanism engendered by a common divinity and morality replaces an egocentric ethnocentrism or pseudospeciation in which other "tribes" are beings of a lesser order.

In terms of the survivor syndrome, not as "mothers of those bastards", the acts of these daughters are portrayed as acts of moral courage: to ensure the continuity of life - which as I have suggested is one of the main themes of the life of Abraham. In the story of the holocaust at Sodom, these daughters-becoming-mothers are the real heroes.

For Abraham, the destruction of the cities in the Plain has a different significance. Unlike Lot's wife, who became a fixed monument to this holocaust, Abraham is transformed into the survivor-witness. Victims of PTSD often suffer from guilt about surviving when others have not or about the things they had to do in order to survive, perhaps like Lot himself. Such "survivor guilt" and "survivor shame" (Lifton 1979; Abramovitch 1986) often has a paralyzing effect in which individuals avoid activities or situations which may arouse recollections of the traumatic events, as if to say like Cain, it is too much to bear (4:13). In cases of frozen or numbed guilt, the individual is unable to confront his guilt; nor is he able to illuminate it and to persevere in that humbling knowledge. The guilty man must act "to restore the order-of-being injured by him through the relation of an active devotion to the world - for wounds of the order-of-being can be healed in infinitely many other places than those at which they were inflicted" (Buber 1965:136).

Abraham, removed from the immediate epicenter of the catastrophe, has a certain distance from the "smoke" and hence perspective. Unlike the inhabitants, he had advance warning. When he had started "bargaining", he had been confident that they were over 50 good men in Sodom; now he learned that there were not even 10. The distance being able to look down allowed him to accept the survivor mission thrust upon him.

The content of the survivor mission is set out in the soliloquy of the Lord: "For I have singled him out, that he may instruct his children and his posterity to keep the way of the Lord by doing what is right and just" (Gen. 18:19). צדק ומשפט (Hebrew: "tsedek umishpat".)[60] Guilt of surviving, as Lifton has shown, need not be paralyzing; it can also be energizing. (Lifton 1971, 1979).

Abraham would therefore feel that he was spared the fate of Sodom for a reason, but if he or his descendants strayed from their divinely invested survivor mission, then they would be liable to the same massive destruction as the Sodomites.

An Image of Ultimate Horror

In the collective memory of the Hebrews the destruction of Sodom and cities of the Plain remained a lasting "image of ultimate horror". It was a tangible proof of the terrible price to be paid for ethical waywardness and social perversion. The theme is stated most dramatically in the book of Deuteronomy 29:21- during Moses' third and final discourse to the children of Israel before his death (but probably reflecting the period of the Exile[61]):

> *The future generations, your children who are to come after you, as also the stranger from a distant country, will see the plagues of that land and the diseases Yahweh will inflict on it, and will exclaim, "Sulphur, salt, scorched earth, the whole land through! No one will sow, nothing will grow, no grass spring ever again. Like this, Sodom and Gomorrah were overthrown, Admah and Zeboiim, which Yahweh overthrew in his anger and his wrath." And all the nations will exclaim "Why has Yahweh treated his land like this? Why this great blaze of anger?" And people will say, "Because they deserted the covenant of Yahweh, the God of their fathers"* (Deut. 29:21-25).

For the later prophets, Sodom and its fate remained an ethical fulcrum, a negative identity of unliveable destruction; the deserving negative fate of those who abandon the moral imperative of the ancestral survivor mission inherited from Abraham, as he saw the smoke rising from the Plain. The apocalytic language of the Prophets uncannily recalls the omnipresent contemporary threat of nuclear devastation, not only killing all the earth's inhabitants but making it unliveable for generations: "a desolation forever" (Zep. 2:9); "never more will anyone live there or be born there from generation to generation" (Is. 13:19-20); "no man will make his home there again"(Jer. 49:18) (cf. also Ez. 16; Jer. 50:40; 23:14; Is. 1:9-10; Amos 4:ll). Isaiah, Jeremiah, Amos, Zephaniah and Ezekiel also express the collective image of total destruction as the dark half of Abraham's survivorhood: "Had Yahweh not left us a few survivors, we should be like Sodom. We should now be like Gomorrah" (Is. 1:9) or "You were like a brand snatched from the blaze". (Amos 4:11).

Mankind, as survivors of the flood via Noah; the Hebrews, in a more personal way, as survivors of Sodom, via Abraham, inherit a survivor's view of reality:

> *If there is a single climatic moment in the Abraham legend − and there may be several - I believe it is when Abraham views these smoking ruins, knowing, as we know what has passed between himself and the Lord, knowing as we*

know, what is to come for Isaac and his descendants, understanding, as Lot
never understands, the true meaning of barrenness, beauty, fruitfulness and
possession.

(Gros Louis 1982:74-5).

Abraham, viewing "the smoke of the land rising like the smoke of the kiln" (19:28), from "the place where he had stood before the Lord" (19:27), is one of the great moments of silence in Scripture. This silence contrasts back to the passive silence in the call to "break out" (12:1-6) and points ahead to his silence at the call to "akeda" (22:1f). It is a silence, however, which is embedded within the confines of the dialogue which preceeded it.

Such is the intent of the phrase, "Next morning, Abraham hurried to the place where he had stood before the Lord" (19:27), as if to continue in action, the words which came before. It is clear that Abraham, unlike the reader of the Text, does not know what has happened to Sodom and the cities of the plain. Rushing to look down, Abraham must have hope and faith that his argument with God was successful; that although "the outrage of Sodom and Gomorrah is so great and their sin so grave" (18:20), if enough good men do not stand aside, then they can withstand and compensate the evils of an entire community.

Now, Abraham watching, seeing, understanding that he has been naive concerning the pervasiveness and reality of human evil. Along with the forcefulness of divine retribution and his own intergenerational survival mission, for Abraham and his image of the goodness of humankind, it was a necessary moment of silent disillusionment.

"One Last Move"

In this hundreth year, (analogous to Levinson's "Age Fifty Transition"), Abraham makes one more move, his last "new start". Leaving the view of the smoking ruins, he moves to the City-Kingdom of Gerar, in the Western Negev. Once again, he carries out a "brother-sister act" with Sarah, and once again wins residency rights. Divine intervention comes this time via a dream, to the king (anticipating the importance of Royal Dreams in the story of Israel), which simultaneously protects Sarah and establishes Abraham's reputation as a intecessor or prophet:

> *But God came to Avimelech in a dream by night and said to him, "You are to die because of the women that you have taken, for she is a married woman." Now Avimelech had not approached her. He said, "O, Lord, will you slay people even innocent? He himself said to me, 'She is my sister!' Morever, she said, 'He is my brother.' When I did this, my heart was blameless and my hands were clean." And God said to him in a dream, "I knew that you did this with a blameless heart, and so I kept you from sinning against Me. That was why I did not let you touch her. But you must intercede for you - to save your life. If you fail to restore her, know that you shall die, you and all that are yours." (20:3-7).*

This is the first dream recorded in Scripture and as such is worthy of special attention. It is tantalizing to speculate in what visual image did "God" appear to the King? Was it in the form of his own Cannanite God-image or was it as one may suggest for the child Samuel, a palpable if unseen voice, or as happens in incubational Temple dreaming, a human image who one knows is "Divine". Unlike the dreams of pharaoh, this dream is virtually lacking in symbolic thinking. Rather in a narrative sequence the main thrust of this dream is to continue the dialogue over the nature of morality and ethical-destructive continuum, began by Abraham before Sodom. If the reader has learned that evil can overwhelm a community, here, one sees that wrongdoing can come about even without evil intent. "I knew you did this with a blameless heart" (20:6).

On the other hand, God's synchronistic saving influence, or "saving grace" may not be immediately (or ever) apparent even it to its beneficiary, (like Chesterton's Father Brown, not so much solving murders as preventing them from happening). Yet blameless heart or not, had the King, even unconsciously, adulterous union with another man's wife, he would be culpable; - not to the husband, as in most legal codes of ancient Near East (Pritchard 1969), but to the Supreme Moral Orderer.

Adultery is not a tort, the wrongful use of another man's property, but a violation of a sacred moral order, with punishment, appropriately, capital.

Dreams, as Jung argued, are not all of a piece but fall into different genres. This dream of the king is what is called a "big dream", a dream like Solomon's legitimizing the Temple on Mt. Moriah, the site of the akeda i.e. one of special collective significance (Lincoln 1936; Kilbourne 1982). A king's dream, like his ritual fault, may have significance for his community as a whole, beyond any personal, private import. Just as a weak king puts the entire kingdom in literal, as well as a magical, danger.

This dream dialogue illustrates two points about biblical notions of identity. The first has to do with the dialectic between collective and personal responsibility, the theme illustrated in the debate over Sodom. If the King has committed a sin, in this case an unconscious ritual fault, his entire kingdom will suffer ("... you shall die, you and all that are yours." 20:7) An individual, especially a representative or symbolic leader, a "king", "president" or "pillar of a society" may commit an individual act which may led to harm for many. The case of David's adultery with Batsheva and its terrifying cover-up is a case in point. The result is that people will be slayed "even though innocent" (20:4).

The second point has to do with identity for oneself and identity for others, one's social role or "persona". For Abraham to become a "navi" or prophet, he must be given recognition as one. In more general terms to consolidate a new identity and social role, one needs public recognition of that new identity and social role. It was in that vein that Abraham's rush to hospitality was understood ("As soon as he saw them, he ran from the entrance of the tents to greet them..." 18:2) for they were the first "others" able to greet him in his new name, Av-raham. In Gerar, he arrives as a defenseless refugee from the holocaust. After this dream, he is publically recognized as a prophet (20:17-18):

> Abraham then prayed to God, and God healed Abimelech and his wife and his
> slave girls so that they bore children..."

This fervent year (Genesis 17-20) concluded with Abraham successfully assuming the role of prophet, mediator between heaven and earth. Although barren himself, he prayed for the fertility and health of Abi-melech and his wives, reaffirming his connection to YHWH, and receiving thereby social recognition of his special divine affiliation. This recognition would have been particularly important to him after his first unsuccessful attempt at mediating for the people of Sodom. Abraham's successful prayers for Abimelech contained the latent suggestion that thus far it was Sarah or Abraham (or both) who were responsible for their own barrenness. At the end of this age 50 transition, Abraham was firmly established as a prophet, with a new name and official rights of residence in the promised land.

Genesis 21 covers the stable period of middle adulthood and recounts three few important marker events: the birth and weaning of Issac, along with the agonizing expulsion of his "other" son; a treaty with the same King of Gerar "not deal falsely with me or my kith and kin, but (will) deal with me and with the land in which you have sojourned as loyally as I have dealt with you" (21:23), along with negotiations concerning Abraham's rights to wells his men have dug; and planting of a tree, a tamarisk at Beersheva (possible a spin off of the treaty), where he "invoked there the name of the Lord, the Everlasting God" (21:33) (Hebrew: "YHWH, el 'olam").

The significance of these marker events, will be discussed, in the next chapter when we return, finally, to our initial concern: How did the first father come to (almost) kill his last remaining son? and What is the meaning of this test within the context of Abraham's life cycle?

CHAPTER EIGHT:
THE AKEDA

Search For Survival

The account of the binding of Isaac, the "akeda", begins with the phrase ויהי אחר הדברים האלה "vayehi akharei hadevarim haeleh", which is translated as "some time afterward" (J.P.S.), "It happened some time later" (Jerusalem Bible) or more literally "and it came to pass after these things" (King James). Despite the modern idiomatic translations, the older King James gives a more faithful account of the Hebrew sense "after these things"; as if "Abraham's sacrifice must not be isolated" (Rouiller 1978:15) but set in some contextual sequence within his life history. The same phrase provides the narrative context for Chapter 15 "It happened after these things, the word of the Lord came unto Abram in a vision saying, 'Hear not, Abram: I am thy shield, and thy exceeding great reward' (King James) in terms of the events of Chapter 14; likewise 39:7; 40:1; 48:1; Joshua 24:29; I Kings 17:17; 21:1. In each case the phrase indicates the passage of time and development of a sequence, something later dependent upon what had gone before.

The Hebrew word הדברים "hadevarim", "things", is also cognate to Hebrew term for "speech", "words" and indeed in most Biblical context, it is used in that meaning as in "word of the Lord" ("devar"). Many Hebrew commentators (Rashi, Targum Jonathan, Tractate Sanhedrin 89) suggest that these "things" refer to previous "speech", such as the word of Satan, akin to the frame story in the book of Job; or boasting between Isaac and Ishmael at the former's weaning feast. But the literal sense is that it is somehow connected with the events in the previous chapter (Rashbam).

Chapter 21 recounts: the birth and weaning of Isaac; the expulsion of Ishmael; the peace treaty with Avimelech King of Gerar; the planting of a tamarisk (Heb. אשל "eshel") at Beersheva; and invoking "there the name of the Lord, the everlasting God" (Heb. אל עולם el olam) (21:33). This period of middle adulthood, during which "Abraham resided in the land of the Philistines a long time" (21:34), represented a stable period, following Levinson's assertion that "the life structure evolves through a relatively orderly sequence during the adult years...of alternating stable (structure building) periods and transitional (structure changing) periods" (Levinson 1978:49).

In this stable period of middle adulthood - Abraham would be in his relative mid-fifties - he had achieved almost everything he would have wished for when he broke away from Haran, trying for a new life structure. He has a son by his own wife, he is an honored resident ("God is with you in everything that you do"), he is able to bring blessings and so make his own and his God's name, great. Despite the realization of much of Abraham's dream, there were some underlying flaws in the life structure and indeed such success inevitably produces change in life structure. This change heralds the end of the stable period and the beginning of a new transition, from middle to late adulthood.

The main conflict in this stable period lay between Abraham and his wife: *Sarah saw the son, whom Hagar the Egyptian had borne to Abraham playing. She said to Abraham, "Cast out that slave-woman and her son, for the son shall not share in the inheritance with my son Isaac". The matter distressed Abraham greatly for it concerned a son of his.* (21:9-11).

In the interests of domestic harmony, and to assure his own pure descent - Ishmael's descent seems tainted by his mother's Egyptian blood - Abraham long before the akeda, is asked to sacrifice his first born son. The argument between Abraham and Sarah, insofar as ancient legal texts may be relevant (ANET; De Vaux 1978; Sarna 1966; Van Seters; Thompson 1974) revolves around Ishmael's legal status. If Ishmael at his birth was recognized as a legitimate heir then he ought not be disinherited even if the legitimate wife bears a child subsequently. On the other hand, as in later Israelite law, if he is only the son of slave, then he remains a slave without rights of inheritance. "The Law of Lipit-Ishtar, about one hundred and fifty years earlier than Hammurabi, stipulates that the offspring of a slave-wife relinquish their inheritance rights in return for their freedom" (Sarna 1966:156), which may be the case at hand. Sarah's claim to disinherit Ishmael is clearly expressed in her use of the term, "son of the slave-women"; as if to suggest that she never recognized him as a legitimate heir.

Despite God's consolation "Do not be distressed over the boy or your slave...I will make a great nation of him, too, for he is your seed" (21:12-13), the loss of Ishmael would have been a major trauma for Abraham. Ishmael is **forced** to adopt the wandering life style which Abram **chose** for himself; while Isaac is suddenly transformed from a younger brother into an only child. It is not surprising that in later life Isaac is twice described at the well of **Beer-lahai-roi** ("Well of the Living One Who see me"), where Hagar had once fled (16:13-14), as if, after the death of his mother, and again after the death of his father (25:11), searching for his lost brother.

With Ishmael gone to his destiny as a "Wild Man" (Bly 1990), Abraham is once again completely dependant upon his only son to provide a sense of continuity or "symbolic immortality" (Lifton 1979). Such a dependence upon a single son in which all the great promises reside is not without "deep ambivalence". How can Abraham be sure that Isaac will carry on his spiritual revolution? How can he be certain that Isaac will believe in the God of his father and be acceptable to Him? How can he be sure that his son will never betray him - as Abram "betrayed" his own father Terah? Wolfenstein (1967) in his study of "The Revolutionary Personality" has argued that when a father rebelled against paternal authority, then his own sons appear all the more potentially disloyal and dangerous - lest they do to him what he did to his own father.

These feelings of dependence, potential betrayal, even lingering guilt over his own break out created a "second crisis of generativity". Despite all he had achieved, with death and mortality becoming increasingly inevitable, he could not be secure in passing on his vision to the next generation. What Abraham needed to do was to allow Isaac to achieve his own independent faith in Abraham's mission, thereby guaranteeing his loyalty and devotion to it.

Moreover, despite his apparent success, Abraham must have become increasingly aware how few of God's promises would be fulfilled in his own lifetime (indeed their very repetition suggests a lingering transgenerational need for reassurance). Despite the peace treaty, he owned no land and lived as a "resident alien" at the whim of local rulers, without legal protection, regarded as a outsider. Despite his prayers, he had hardly become the instrument of God's blessing and he had no spiritual disciples, certainly none outside his own family camp. Moreover, instead of living up to his new name, "father of many nations" he had fathered only two sons, one of whom he had sent off and the other was still a child - one liable to be dominated by a doting mother. Perhaps Isaac would in the end be as unacceptable as Ishmael had been!

Take Your Son...

Many commentators (Kierkegaard 1954; Auerbach 1953; Wilson 1954; Van Seters 1975) describe this last call as a "command" and Abraham's response, a test of obedience. Such an interpretation, however, does not fit the Hebrew phrase, קח נא 'kakh na". It is usually translated as "take" which would be the meaning of "kakh" alone. The addition of "na" indicates that it is not a command but rather a request. In Genesis alone there are 25 examples of the "na" construction but even if we restrict our survey to those within Abraham's narrative (12:13; 13:9; 13:14; 15:5; 16:2; 19:2; 24:2); each is clearly a request, often an unusual request[62] which might perhaps be translated "please take" or "Why not take". Indeed given the history of their relation, Abraham's silence here cannot mean blind obedience to an all-powerful God. Before Sodom, Abraham was very capable of striving with God, arguing for the lives of a city full of sinners - would he not fight for the life of his blameless child! Abraham's decision to comply with the request was his own. His silence here contrasts with his silence at the first call. Then he went out lured by promises, now he must set out with a devotion based on an autonomous decision to follow the Lord without reward and indeed the seeming betrayal of all that was promised.

The narrator or redactor places a frame around the story with the second phrase "God put Abraham to the test"[63] (22:1) (J.P.S.), or "God did tempt Abraham" in the King James version (cf. I Kings 10:1; Judges 6:39; Deut. 6:16; Judges 2:22; 3:1,4; etc.). In most cases it is Israel who test God's patience or God who sets Israel as a nation to the test, but this is the only case in which a single individual is so tried by the Lord. "When it is known from the beginning that this was a test of Abraham's fidelity, the reader is then free from the necessity of tragedy and irreparable horror "(Gonzalez 1967:12). As Sarna (1966) notes, there is no explicit renunciation of human sacrifice in the story, because the narrative implicitly rejects associating God with human sacrifice. As a revolutionary founder, he is able to do what no one else is allowed to do. Therefore the akeda is an exception, an aberration, not a command, never a rule to follow. The reader knows that it is a test, "the last trial"; but for it to be a trial, Abraham cannot know. For Abraham, the call to Moriah is "the story of a choice" (Gonzalez 1967:125).

And the temptation? Not that he would refuse to "sacrifice" (Latin, lit. "make holy") his son but rather, given a revolutionary founder's filicidal ambivalence, that **he would want to kill him**.

There is something in Abraham's action which defies logical thinking. Emil Fackenheim, himself a Holocaust survivor, rabbi and philosopher, has put the position clearest in his essay "Abraham and the Kantians" (in Encounters Between Judaism and Modern Philosophy). He contrasts Kant's absolute logic and categorical imperative, which insists that logically Abraham cannot go to offer up his son at Moriah. According to the Kantians, one can be sure, absolutely, that human sacrifice is morally wrong. One, however, can not be sure that the voices one hears are truly the word of God. In this case, since the voice violates an absolute moral imperative, one can say with certainty that the voice is not the Voice, the word of God, but demonic (cf. Hebrew midrashim on this theme). Abraham is logically forced to choose between doing what is right and the word of the alleged God. According to rationality, he must choose the former and remain home.

The logical paradox is deepened since the request to offer up his son negates all the previous promises, "the complete nullification of the covenant and the frustration forever of all hope for posterity" (Sarna 1966:163). If he reasonably considered the implication of what he was called on to do, he should have cried out at the monstrous injustice, as he had protested the fate of the cities in the plain. Surely Abraham ought to have defended the life of his loving son from such a "Jealous God" as he had argued so vigorously for the life of strangers and sinners of Sodom. During the three-day march (which clearly indicated that it was not an impulsive act), Abraham must have had much opportunity to consider such arguments. The text, however, tells us nothing of this but shows us only his exceptional, eloquent silence, of one who is not afraid to speak out.

Abraham's first response, הנני "Heneni", "Here I am" became the standard Biblical response to a divine call (Ex. 3:4; I Sam 3:4; Is. 58:9; Gen 46:2; cf. also Gen. 27:1; 37:13; II Sam 1:7). The Hebrew gives the force of readiness and sense of place (cognate to הנה "henei" Hebrew for "here"), as though ready to hear and take my stand. The phrase "heneni" is repeated twice more in the 19 verses which comprise the story. During the long walk, Isaac suddenly turns to his companion and says, "Father!" to which Abraham answers virtually as he had answered the Voice, "heneni", which J.P.S. translates "Yes, my son" (22:7) but King James, more accurately conveying the "Leitwort", the repeated verbal motif, "Here am I" (with emphasis on the "am" instead of the early "Here I am"). Contrast two other scenes in Genesis in which a son responds to his father, "heneni": "When Isaac was old and his eyes were too dim to see, he called his older son Esau and said to him, "My son." He answered, "Here I am". (27:1) ; "Israel said to Joseph, "Your brothers are pasturing at Schechem. Come I will send you to them". He answered, "I am ready" (37:13). The contrast implies then, that on the way to Moriah, there is a reversal of roles, the son asking the question and the father expressing his readiness to respond.

The third and final "heneni" occurs at the climactic moment of the sacrifice: "And Abraham picked up the knife to slay his son. Then an angel of the Lord called to him from heaven: "Abraham, Abraham!" And he answered; "Here I am" (22:10-11) in an exact parallel of his first response. The call "Abraham, Abraham!" and his reply "Here I am" ready, in place, to hear what is asked, provide the inner frame of the first 11 verses of the text.

Another repeated word is "together" "two of them together" or "both together" (Heb. יחדיו שניהם "shneihem yakhdav"). The word יחדיו "yakhdav" first appears in the narrative context of the separation of Lot from Abraham after their return from Egypt: "so that the land could not support them staying together; for their possessions were so great that they could not remain together" (13:6). The land and their possessions do not allow the two to remain "yakhdav", together. In the previous chapter's story of the treaty, the text states, "and the two of them made a pact" hinting that although they "cut a treaty" they remained separate, untogether. After Abraham has left his servants behind:

> Abraham took the wood for the burnt offering and put it on his son Isaac. He himself took the firestone and the knife; and the two walked off together. Then Isaac said to his father Abraham, "Father!" And he answered, "Yes, my son." And he said, "Here are the firestone and the wood; but where is the sheep for the burnt offering?" And Abraham said, "God will see to the sheep for His burnt offering, my son." And the two of them walked on together (22:6-8)

The Hebrew for the "two walked on together" and "the two walked off together" is identical, a verbal echo hidden by the idiomatics of the translation. Once again King James tries to preserve the text more closely, translating both as "They went both of them together". The parallel of "both together" suggests a contrast between the first and repeated phrase. The first "both together" is a physical companionship; while the second hints at a spiritual companionship, a deeper unity, with a shared sense of togetherness.

Leaving the servants behind means that the akeda is a private event. There will be no neutral observers, only participant-observers. Second, in transferring the wood to Isaac, he makes him into a sort of beast of burden, reserving the transformative fire and knife for himself. Isaac's question, is evocative - even the great German scholar Gunkel could write "The narrator has tears in his eyes" (quoted in Rouiller 1978:21). Recent scholars have discovered that the entire akeda story itself displays chiastic parallels (cf. Avishur in Weinfeld et al 1982:142) which pivot on Isaac's question, as if to give a central pivotal place.

The question, however, allows us to infer certain aspects of the relationship between son and father. First, it reveals that this is not the first time father and son have set out, the two of them together, to make a burnt offering. Isaac is clearly familiar with the requirements and details of such a rite. Second, Isaac has achieved the age of reason. He is able to infer, from its absence, the necessity of what is missing. Such cognitive ability puts him at least at the stage of "concrete operations:" or possibly "formal operations" in Piaget scheme of cognitive development. Although Isaac's age, as we noted, is deliberately left vague, we suggest that he is at the very least seven or eight and probably a few years older[65], at least 12 or 13. The question also suggests an open, easy relationship in which the son can ask his father for information. Finally, Isaac's question, with its logical structure, is a contrast to Abraham's transcendence of logic as witness in his answer, "God will provide..." and indeed in his silent persistence.

"Abraham looked up and saw the place from afar" (22:4) or more literally in King James, "Then on the third day, Abraham lifted up his eyes, and saw the place afar off". The Hebrew equivalent of "lift up his eyes and see:" "vayisa einav vayar" וישא עיני וירא is also a phrase which occurs frequently in Genesis: "And Lot lifted up his eyes and beheld all the plain of Jordan..." (13:10); And he (Abraham) lifted up his eyes and looked and lo, three men stood by him" (18:2); 24:64-5 and he lifted up his eyes and saw... "And Rebecca lifted up her eyes and when she saw Isaac, she lighted off the camel. (24:63-4); "And they (Joseph's brothers) lifted up their eyes and looked and behold a company of Ishmaelites..." (37:25). (all King James). The sense of the phrase carries a sense of the unexpected of seeing something for the first time, or in a new light.

The "both together" phrasing has one final contrast. At the end of the incident, after the ram is sacrificed in place of ("takhat") Isaac, and promises repeated in the presence of father and son, "Abraham then returned to his servants and they departed together ("yakhdav") for Beersheva (22:19). Isaac is not mentioned "together" with Abraham and he does not appear again until he meets Rebekah at the Well of the Seeing God (24:62-67). The plain sense of the text is that Abraham left Isaac on the top of the mountain, not abandoned but left to contemplate in isolation the terrible event, which bound man and God on the Mountain where God will see/shall be seen.[66] Indeed the next time Isaac appears he is described as as going out "lasuakh" לשוח which is usually translated as "walking" but as King James and J.P.S. versions say may mean "to meditate", although the meaning of the Hebrew is uncertain. Leaving Isaac to meditate on the akeda served to break the dangers of a maternal symbiosis by forcing him to come to grips with the destiny he had now inherited, by himself.

Abraham is forced to choose between devotion to his son and loyalty to his God. In a sense, throughout his life history, he has repeatedly chosen God and His destiny over family attachments. In this sense, the akeda "seems less a climatic moment and more like a coda, a final refrain that recalls for us the themes of Abraham's life" (Gros Louis 1982:75). Only having lost Isaac does Abraham receive him back away, with all promises reaffirmed, almost as if he were brought back from the dead (cf. Midrashim on this theme in Spiegel's seminal work, **The Last Trial**). This is what is miraculous about akeda, that having lost all, he is given it all back again.

There are a number of other latent, even unconscious factors, which may have influenced Abraham's choice of God over son. One issue we have discussed concerned passing on the new tradition of a spiritual revolutionary. Another murky issue concerns Isaac's true paternity. Although Genesis nowhere overtly suggests that Abraham is not the true father of Isaac, there are many questionable aspects concerning his conception. The Biblical account, for example, does not use the normal formulae such as "Adam knew his wife Eve and she conceived and bore Cain (4:1) cf. 4:7 or "And he cohabited (literally "went in" as in King James) with Hagar and she conceived" (16:4). Rather the text uses a peculiar phrasing, "The Lord took note (or visited) of Sarah as He had promised and the Lord did for Sarah as He had spoken" (21:1). Nowhere is Abraham's active role mentioned. More disconcerting was the time Sarah spent in Avimelech's palace. Her earlier encounter as pharaoh's concubine, it seems evident, included sexual relations.

At Gerar, the evidence that Sarah did not have such sexual relations is the dream and word of Avimelech "What have you done to us? What wrong have I done to you that you should bring so great a guilt upon me and my kingdom? You have done to me things that ought not to be done." (20:9). Even more troubling is the question of when Isaac was conceived. Was Isaac already "in utero" prior to Sarah's night in Gerar? If so, then Abraham repeated the pattern of paternal neglect, "abandoning" his unborn child and pregnant woman at a time when she ought rightly be under his special protection. If Sarah was not yet pregnant, then one can imagine a lingering hidden doubt that perhaps, Isaac was not his, but a bastard son. Such suspicions, unconscious and undoubtedly untrue, would increase Abraham's love/hate ambivalence. Agreeing to offer up his son might also have given expression to unconscious hostility toward Isaac, while at the same time relieving him of any guilt for these aggressive impulses since the request to slay Isaac came not from himself but from his God.[67]

"Chosen to Survive"

This traumatic encounter with death and his father's filicidal tendencies made Isaac into a survivor (Lifton 1971). Thus Isaac came away from Moriah much as Abraham had come away from the smoking furnace of Sodom, with a survivor's sense of having been saved, chosen for some special purpose. Left alone on the mountain and at the Well of the Seeing God, Isaac had solitude to meditate upon his own survivor mission.

The blessing which the angel bestows ("I will bestow My blessing upon you and make your descendants as numerous as the stars of heaven and the sands of the seashore; and your descendants shall seize the gates of their foes. All the nations of the earth shall bless themselves by your descendants, because you have obeyed My command" (22:17-18) are formally addressed to Abraham, but he had heard all these promises before. For Isaac, there are his first revelation and specify the grand promise of his survivor mission to carry on the spiritual revolution of the God of his Father. Isaac at akeda, was bound to God, the God of Abraham.

Although many commentators see the akeda as a sacrifical drama between an old man and his young son, at least one Hebrew tradition suggests an alternative. In an attempt to link up the akeda with the death of Sarah, in the next chapter, Sarah is said to have died from fright and despair at the thought of the loss of her only son. Her frantic searching ended in a grief-induced demise and left her dead in Beersheva. The upshot of this midrashic tradition is not only to include a mother's natural feelings into the akeda and family dynamics perspective (marriages do often break up and become dysfunctional upon the death of a child) but to place Isaac right in the middle of his mid-life crisis at 37. Since Isaac was born when his mother was about 90 Biblical years (17:17... "can Sarah bear a child at ninety?") and dies at the age of 127 (23:1) then if the akeda scenario killed her, Isaac would be 37. In terms of "Biblical Years" as applied to Abraham, it would place him in relative terms of a modern life cycle at 18.5, on the threshold between early adulthood and late adolescence. The older ages for Isaac emphasize how little Isaac was the passive helpless victim but some sort of participant, willing to offer himself up. In intergenerational terms, the akeda occurs in father's transition between late to late late adulthood, while his son just about to become a man of his own right, when intergenerational tension is at its greatest.

For Abraham, the akeda enacted the symbolic death of Isaac as merely a biological son but confirmed him in the role of prophet-successor chosen by God to carry out their covenant [68] in this divinely inspired "psychodrama".

Abraham resolved the paradox of revolutionary continuity. The akeda demonstrated God's confirmation of his beloved son as His spiritual successor, fusing biological with spiritual continuity. For Isaac, it was a sort of "creative trauma", a ritual ordeal or initiation, into a relationship with the divine. It signaled his future role as a prophet of his father's God, who might be his own God, the God of Abraham, who would become the God of Isaac... (Did the Lord really need the test to know that Abraham was worthy? - or did He need for Abraham to know, in the presence of his son, that he **was** indeed worthy; and/or to show Isaac the son that he too might also be worthy?)

For Abraham, himself on the edge of old age, he could rest confident, in this second crisis of generativity to "keep the way of the Lord by doing what is right and just in order that the Lord may bring about for Abraham what he has promised him" (18:19).

The akeda is the culminating event in Abraham's spiritual career, the last time he had any direct contact with God. The tension between divinity and family, between spirituality and kinship, is finally resolved at this "last call". Choosing God, he received his son, and more, God's choosing his son. Abraham proved to himself (and to Isaac) that he did not hold his son above his God. In doing so Abraham sacrificed his son, not as a burnt offering but as a prophet in the service of God. He had impressed upon Isaac the need for emphatic detachment to and passionate reaffirmation of family ties while maintaining an intense personal relationship with God. Thus ends Abraham's spiritual career; but his life history is not yet completed.

CHAPTER NINE:
FINAL RECONCILIATION

Old Age in the Bible

The akeda (22:1-19) completes Abraham's spiritual odyssey, finishing the search for place, progeny and God begun in Haran (12:1). As we noted in the introduction, the chapters 12-22 form a chiastic structure within a literary unit, the years of Abraham's adult life which were shaped by his relation with his God. In the remaining chapters (23-25) God does not appear to Abraham, and from the viewpoint of his spiritual odyssey, especially after the akeda the following chapters are anticlimatic. On the other hand, chapters 23 and 24 include some of the finest examples of storytelling through dialogue in the Bible. Yet in terms of the unfolding of Abraham's life history, the relative lack of suspense and conflict and the resolution of outstanding issues of late adulthood (and late late adulthood) are part of a successful aging process. Indeed, Abraham final years become the Biblical standard of of a good old age.

Sternberg has discussed the contrasting meanings of "old age" in Genesis. Concerning Abraham, he writes:

> ...the first patriarch is yet the first character to receive the epithet: "Abraham was old, advanced in years, and the Lord had blessed Abraham in everything" (24:1). "Everything" we soon learn, includes not only great wealth but also a new lease of procreativity and the retention of all spiritual powers... with his characteristic wisdom, foresight and fairness...even the parting from Abraham sketches an idyllic picture. It leaves an impression of the most natural death ("in a good old age, an old man and full of years"); familial harmony between the sons ranged in the hierarchical order predetermined by the father ("Isaac and Ishmael his sons buried him"); and, to screw down the antithesis, a reunion with the proper mate ("Sarah his wife") in their own cave of "Machpelah".
> Epithetic old age thus associated with all blessings of character and fortune, it becomes their overt metonymy. Surface and depth appear to establish in concert the type of the Departing Patriarch. So the reader naturally looks forward to the recurrence of this typal precedent in the next generation. But history does not repeat itself, except to dissociate external from internals. Contrary to expectation, "Isaac was old and his eyes were dim so that he

could not see" (27:1) turns out to be a prologue to a very different tale. Here old age goes neither with admirable character nor with happiness and success but with failing powers all round, notably spiritual as well as physical decay ("blindness").

(Sternberg 1985:350-1)

Other Biblical characters whose lives are described in any detail mostly have wretched old ages. Jacob suffers from interminable mourning over his lost son and even after the unexpected reunion he says (to pharaoh): "The years of my sojourn (on earth) are 130. Few and hard have been the years of my life, nor do they come up to the life span of my fathers" (47:9). Moses, forbidden from entering the promised land, dies alone - "to this day no one has found his grave" (Deut. 34:6). David, after his sin with Bathsheba, suffers the loss of children: the infant son of the adulterous union; the revenge killing of Amnon by Abshalom (lit. av-shalom - "father-peace" but perhaps also metaphorically ironically "father-goodbye") after the former raped his sister Tamar; and finally the humiliation of Abshalom's rebellion and death after which David narrowly avoids the fate of Jacob's interminable mourning: "My son Absalom! Would that I had died in your place..." (II Sam. 19:2) His last days are tormented by further rebellions, pestilence, struggles over succession and even his last words (I Kings 2:1-9) are full of malice and resentment, failure to reconcile those disperate parts of his personality. In this final period, God abandons him: Joseph Heller in his fanciful but textually faithful account of David, **God Knows** gives voice to his ego despair:

In solitude, I was raging at the Lord, seething with scornful belligerence toward the Lord, and spoiling for a fight with Him. I really could not keep my temper. I wanted to have it out with Him, I was ready to curse God and die. But He would not take me on. I never did get from Him the justification I wanted for the death of the child. I received instead the answer I least expected.

Silence.

It is the only answer I have got from Him since.

(Heller 1985:370-1)

Scripture does not recount any contact between God and Abraham after the akeda, but it seems to imply the converse of David, not that God abandoned Abraham but that having blessed Abraham in all things they had said all that they needed to say to each other.

Reconciling the old and new heritage

When Abram "broke out" of his old life structure to "become his own man" as part of his mid-life transition, the break appeared decisive and irrevocable. Led by a new kind of divine vision, Abram had abandoned an aging father to die in Kharan. He had also rejected his father's authority over him, by leaving his father and foresaking his father's gods. The process of self-creation or self affirmation was symbolized by taking on the new name Avraham, indicative of his new status as a Father in his own right. Ironically, Avraham could only start becoming "Our Father Avraham" outside the physical sphere of his father's influence. The text (22:20) implies that there was no contact between Abraham and his father's family until after the akeda. Now firmly established in the patriarchal role, having resolved the twin crises of faith, Abraham is prepared to reconcile with his past, his Mesopotamian heritage.

The developmental tasks of Abraham's old age were final steps to assure physical continuity. "The death of Sarah is the occasion for acquiring a family sepulcher. Then, Isaac has to be married to ensure the succession of the line" (Sarna 1966:166). Having achieved a successful succession, Abraham, still sexually potent, is able to father another six children and send them off without any of the apparent guilt and torment which marked Ishmael's expulsion, as it is written: "Abraham willed all that he owned to Isaac; but to the sons of Abraham by concubines Abraham gave gifts while he was still living and he sent them away from his son Isaac eastward, to the land of the East." (25:5-6).[69]

The instructions to his "senior servant" (often identified with Eliezer (15:2) in Jewish tradition) clearly reveal Abraham's dual desire for continuity with **and** separation from his father's family. Isaac's return to Mesopotamia would threaten the entire spiritual enterprise of Abraham's descendants in Canaan. On the other hand, cousin marriage with family from the "old country" would ensure an endogamy of pure descent.

Finally, the entire instructions are sworn 'under the thigh of Abraham', presumably on or near his genitals, sacred symbols of the covenant and his power of reproduction. Through this solemn act (cf. 47:29), Abraham impressed upon his senior servant how in going off to seek a proper wife for Isaac, he was symbolically carrying Abraham's seed in his hand.

The selection of a bride from "from my own land and my own kinfolk" (24:4) was an elegant solution to the dilemma of finding an appropriate wife for Isaac. It perpetuates the family tradition of close kin marriages, guards against intermarriage (exogamy) and hence assures pure lineal descent. At the same time, it allows

Abraham, in his new life structure in Canaan, to re-establish ties family with his kin. In this way, he guarded against a regressive regression to the pagan gods of Mesopotamia, as well as intermingling with the indigenous cults of the Canaanites.

The marriage of Isaac and Rebekah was doubly pleasing. Isaac was healed from the grief of his mother's death and Abraham lived to see his twin grandchildren attain the age of fifteen. He was also able to acknowledge kinship with his brother's family and thereby heal the rift with his father's clan, completing the cycle of the denial and ultimate reaffirmation of family ties.

Abraham's need to reestablish and reconcile with his Mesopotamian kin is highlighted in the puzzling phrases which God gives, assuring Abraham of a long life and a good death: "You shall go to your fathers in peace" (15:15); at his death it is said "He was gathered to his kin" (25:7). These phrases cannot be literally accurate. Abraham's father died in Mesopotamia as did most of his kin. Some archeologists speculate the phrase may refer to various communal forms of burial, such as at the family tomb, or other arrangements revealed in Ezekiel 37 "valley of dry bones" or other arrangements, such as secondary burial revealed by archeological excavation. Even if anachronistic (van Rad 1976), these phrases echo Abraham's need for symbolic continuity, including a final reconciliation with his Mesopotamian heritage.

"The Death and Divorce of Sarah"

The death report of Sarah follows the akeda and, as noted, a midrash seek to link the two events. Practically one could hardly expect the marriage to survive such an event. However, close attention to the text suggests that by the akeda, and certainly at the time of Sarah's death, the couple had become estranged and were, in fact living apart. At the end of the akeda, Abraham returns, without Isaac, to the land of the Philistines to Beersheva (22:19). Sarah dies "in Kiriath-arba - now Hebron - in the land of Canaan; and Abraham proceeded to mourn for Sarah and bewail her" (23:2). The Hebrew word ויבא "vayavo" here translated as "proceeded" normally carries the implication of movement, motion, while other translations suggest "went" or "went in" a corresponding to the suggestion in the Hebrew that Abraham arrived from some other place, presumably Beersheva, about 50 km away, which is the opinion of classic medieval Hebrew commentators, Rashi, and Ibn Ezra. The Hebrew text has a further peculiarity in the word ולבכתה "velevakhta", "bewail her" or "grieve for her". The root of the word derives from "to cry, to weep" and the literal meaning is perhaps "to cry over her" (Ibn Ezra).

In the Hebrew text, the middle letter "kaf" is written in miniature, which has been symbolically understood as indicating that his grief was likewise lessened. Pious interpreters suggest that Abraham was not fully grief stricken because Sarah lived a long full life, but I suggest that in fact his grief was restrained since for many years he has lived in the land of Philistines, while she remained in the other residence in the land of Canaan. Again although literary sequence clearly places the union with Keturah, after the marriage of Isaac, it is not in improbable that their liason actually pre-dated Sarah's death.

If one reviews the relationship between Abraham and Sarah, one can suggest multiple causes for the marital breakdown. Unlike Isaac and Rebekah, about whom Scripture says "and he loved her" (24:67), no such phrase appears concerning Abraham and Sarah. On two occasions Abraham got rid of Sarah and indeed, unlike the King of Sodom, only she could say, "It is I who made Abram rich" (14:23). The search for surrogate motherhood only brought rancor and overt conflict: "The wrong done me is your fault! I myself put my maid in your bosom; now that she sees she is pregnant, I am lowered in her esteem. The Lord decide between you and me." (16:5) as does the promise of their own child: (17:12-15) arguing over who laughed. Moreover, Sarah clearly implies that Abraham is impotent sexually. Again she gets her way when Ishmael and Hagar are chased out of the encampment. In these episodes, Abraham usually defers to Sarah, avoiding an open clash. Just as it is hard to imagine a mother condoning the akeda, it is likely that Abraham harbored lasting resentment for the expulsion of Ishmael. The last recorded conversation is

Sarah's expulsion order: "Cast out that slave women and her son, for the son of that slave shall not share in the inheritance with my son Isaac" (21:10). Note that Sarah does not even refer to either Ishmael or Hagar by name but only by function or role. It takes a further and odd revelation to ensure that Abraham will carry out her command - ironically forcing Ishmael to experience what Abram did, leaving father, kindred and native land. Moreover, as argued above, one of the secondary gains of the akeda was to offset maternal influence or symbiosis.

Sarah as a doting mother would be likely to overprotect and overindulge her son of promise, which would stunt Isaac's spiritual development and undercut his own sense of independence and autonomy. In any case, chronic conflict, clash of values and temperament probably contributed to the marital breakdown long before Abraham proceeded to mourn for his first wife.

"Tombs as Symbols"

The death of Sarah, did, however provide an opportunity to acquire a foothold in the land of Canaan. As a resident alien (**ger vetoshav**) he "labored under a legal disadvantage. The alien could not normally acquire land, and he is usually classed in Biblical literature, along with the orphan and the widow, among the oppressed of society" (Sarna 1966:166-7). Thus he insisted and needed special permission to acquire permanent title to land. As a stranger in the land his position was always precarious. He had won residence rights in Gerar by tricks and divinely inspired dream and later had his position ratified in a further treaty, which may have allowed him "arboreal rights", the right to plant a tree (21). At Hebron, he again shows his characteristic deference to authority; bowing twice, paying the full price, **without** bargaining. It is perhaps significant that he deals not with a Canaanite (cf. Gen 34) but with another immigrant, resident alien presumably from the Hittite homeland in central Anatolia. (de Vaux 1978; Sarna 1966).

The presence of Biblical Hittites remains "a historical riddle", although a number of treaties between Egypt and Hittites (ANET 1955:199-203) do suggest that the area of the HolyLand was an arena of conflict which ultimately fell under the Egyptian sphere of influence. The importance of the purchase, including the legalistic aspect of the discussion and summary: "So Ephron's land in Machpelah, near Mamre - the field with its cave and all the tree anywhere within the confines of that field - passed to Abraham as his possession, in the presence of the Hittites, of all who entered the gate of his town" (24:17-18) was the legitimate acquisition of a permanent piece of the promised land in his lifetime.

The ancestral tomb which Abraham bought for his family - where he himself was buried - as well as his his wife, son, daughter-in-law, grandson and wife and even great grandson, Joseph, may have functioned as an ancestral tomb descibed by Maurice Block for the Merina of Highland Madagascar. As in Abraham's descent group, such tombs are the main focus of ritual and family identity, symbolzing his connection with his ancestral land ("tanindraza"). Bloch (1971:136-7) describes how a person "feels he belongs in a more significant way to his 'tanindrazana' than he does to the place where he lives. In this way, he feels assured of a place in a traditional, good order...where relations are fixed, where anxiety about the behavior of others is therefore non-existent...(at) a time of violent social change, when repeatedly, acquired status, power and wealth were continually redistributed and the only permanent, reliable relations and roles were those associated with the defunct traditional order. In fact, the link with the tanindrazana constitutes the element of continuity in a changing situation..." For the Merina, as for the ancient Hebrews, the tomb was the most vital link with an apparently unchanging moral order, with other kinsmen and hence with Abraham and his mission. Like ancient Hebrews, who brought the bones of Jacob and later Joseph to the ancestral tomb, the Merina and other Malagasy make extraordinary efforts to bring back the bones of those who have been buried away (Abramovitch 1975). The worst fate, or "bad death" is when bones become unavailable for the ancestral tomb, as when a person drowns and his body never recovered. During the wandering of Isaac, Jacob and even more during the time in Egypt, the ancestral tomb of Machpelah served as the symbolic focus of the unity of the Hebrews (cf. "all kinship relations depend on links through the dead...based on having a common forebearer in an ascending generation" (Bloch 1971:167)). It served as the geographical and cultic ritual focus of a sense of an ancestral "home" land - a place where one really belonged. It also was the concrete expression of the reality of Abraham's spiritual odyssey.

Abraham had achieved a more secure permanent identity in Canaan - he had planted a tree, built altars, cut treaty, bought a field and family sepulchre, achieved recognition as a a prince and a prophet, "and the Lord blessed Abraham in all things" (24:1). Overcoming his early psychogenic impotence he is able to father six more sons (and perhaps more daughters/cf. Controversy whether the passage 24:1 "blessed in all things" includes daughters or not) by Keturah. There remains some controversy over Keturah's identity. One Rabbinic tradition associates her with Hagar, suggesting that the Hebrew word "keturah" might be a name of endearment meaning "sweet smelling" literally from the root, "incense". In view of Abraham's instructions concerning Isaac, it seems unlikely that she is local Canaanite but rather local born daughter of one of his household and so, a camp insider. This relation seems to heal the wounds of his relation with Hagar. In this case, he is able to have many sons by a subordinate wife, and grant them gifts, which he was unable to give to Ishmael, so here too one sense an inner reconciliation and peace.

The last chapters of Abraham's life history in Chapters 23-25 describe a successful transition from mid to late adulthood, achieving a sense of continuity and contentment. Abraham remained the Biblical exemplar of a successful and fertile aging; and a model for a good death: "And Abraham breathed his last, dying at a good ripe age, old and contented," buried by both his sons in his cave (25:8) he had himself purchased. Who, in his life cycle, could ask for more?

CHAPTER TEN:
CONCLUSION: THE PSYCHOLOGY OF
SPIRITUAL REVOLUTION

"Intimations of mystery are what the twentieth century needs".

Storr 1986:183

In this appreciation of Abraham as **The First of Fathers**, I have utilized an idiographic or clinical approach of the intensive case study. Along the way, I have occasionally suggested that some of Abraham's conflicts and transformations may apply to the life history of other spiritual revolutionaries. In this concluding chapter, I wish to briefly formulate some of these hypotheses and to move to a nomothetic task of empirically verifiable principle about spiritual revolution. My clinical case study approach goes against the received dogma of most science, including social science, which tries to move from statistically valid general theories to specific cases. The clinical approach starts in the opposite direction, with the individual, and assumes that the universal must first be discerned in the particular.

It is striking that some of the most fertile innovators in psychology based their theories on intense observation of single individuals and indeed, Jean Piaget, Sigmund Freud, Melanie Klein, B.F. Skinner, Charles Darwin among others, derived key insights from studying, or treating their own children.

If innovation in psychology derives from being a parent, then, "the higher reaches of abstract thought require long periods of solitary concentration which are incompatible with married life" (Storr 1988:266). Anthony Storr goes on to note that many great philosophers neither married, nor fathered children. "Most lived alone for the greater part of their lives" (op. cit.).

Spiritual revolution, I suspect, combines aspects of psychological and philosophical innovation since it must deal with how men may live **and** with absolute **truth** and transcendent meaning. As a result, the spiritual revolutionary is likely to have both intensive family relations, especially with "spiritual sons" or disciples and extended periods of intense isolation.

The innovator must break away from "his father's house", his father's God and religion. Often traumatic event or personal tragedy will jar him out of a complacent existence and force him to confront the universal dilemmas concerning death, suffering, evil and redemption. His personal quest will lead him to formulate a vision of reality which concerns not only himself, but all humanity.

The period of isolation may be preceded or punctuated by encounters with a variety of rival religious traditions. These encounters serve to enrich and stimulate the religious imagination and may, as suggested for Abraham, serve as the raw material for a creative synthesis, the coming together of the opposites. At some moment, a "peak experience" or revelation crystallizes the new vision and the individual as a "lonely man of faith" undergoes a mystical experience which embues him with an overwhelming, irresistible sense of purpose: to communicate his vision and its message to others, indeed often to all who may hear. The communication is almost always verbal, by word of mouth or in direct dialogue. Much of religious teachings consist of **written** accounts of these oral teachings which necessarily institutionalize and often fossilize the revolutionary content of the spiritual message of the founder. As mentioned at the outset, written text must be interpreted and therefore cannot have the direct and decisive impact of directed address. Yet, recording the words of the spiritual revolutionary and his disciples is the major manner of ensuring continuity.

Herein lies the tension between innovation and tradition, between the new and the known, the fresh and the old which comprises the crisis of generativity for the revolutionary.

The crisis is symbolized in the new identity and often new name and title which the founder assumes. Such an identity is based on a rejection of his father and tradition.

The rebel must necessarily mistrust his own disciples - as if to say "How can I trust my 'children' not to abandon me and my teachings, as I abandoned those of my fathers?" The extent to which the spiritual revolutionary is able to successful and creatively resolve this crisis of continuity may determine the lasting success of his mission. Ultimately, then, there must be some sort of reconciliation between the older and newer heritage. John the Baptist tries to formulate his radical religious revitalization movement in terms of an older purer tradition when he says to his fellows in Luke and Mathew: "Do not think of telling yourselves, 'We have Abraham for our father', because I tell you, God can raise children for Abraham from these stones" (Luke 3:8; cf. Matthew 3:9). Here John the Baptist is undoing the interdependence of biological and spiritual descent, claiming "true sons of Abraham" are only those of the Spirit. Certainly, whatever mentoring the spiritual seeker may have received, it is clear that one of his great tasks is the mentoring of others, selecting, guiding, bringing out the best in them. Likewise, as Toynbee and others suggest, when the would be innovator returns to society from his period of isolation (as often as not in the desert, an ideal location for introspection and experiencing timelessness), he must convince at least one other person of the validity of his vision; that one will remain a confirming mirror of the validity of his inner conviction during all the adversity to follow. Without such a confirming experience, the would be innovator may be so "cut off" from society as to appear mad.

The belief of one other is what assures the revolutionary of his sanity and the possibility of the success of his mission. This confirming individual often forms the core of the successor community. It seems clear that spiritual seekers set out during transitional periods in their adult development: Abraham in mid-life crisis; Jesus during an age thirty transition; Confuscius apparently at age 50 transition ("At fifty, I knew the biddings of heaven"); Tolstoy at the bounding of mid and late adulthood. Except for those who die young, before the transition to the second half of life, the tumultous transition is followed by a stable period of consolidation in both personal and social spheres. Yet the innovator may persist in certain paradoxical acts which are prerogatives of the mythic founder, acts like the akeda which are **not** models for his spiritual descendant. The peaceful manner of death often clashes with the struggles round his spiritual succession, reflecting the relative success of resolving the communal crisis of generativity.

Joseph Campbell has written that dead divinities become consuming demons. The perennial task of the spiritual revolutionary in such times is to use the mystery and disorder, to "spur man to discovery, to the creation of new hypotheses which bring order and pattern to the maze of phenomena" (Storr 1988:172-3). In this way, cynicism, power and alienation may give way to hope, generosity and togetherness; and so inspire men and woman with a new vision which makes living seem worthwhile.

EPILOGUE

Man of today resists the Scriptures because he cannot endure revelation. To endure revelation is to endure this moment full of possible decisions, to respond to and be responsible for every moment.

- Martin Buber (in Friedman 1983:73)

Abraham and the Paths of Peace

The story of Abraham deals with a dilemma concerning ownership and residence of the land, which originally belonged to someone else - a dilemma which is at the heart of the Israel-Palestine conflict. The stories about firstborns and laterborns, "pure" descent and tainted bastards, contingent or unconditional promises all deal with the conflict engendered by occupying a land which is your by promise but not by "birthright".

Appropriately, Abraham is very much alive and in contemporary Israeli political imagination. Indeed, he is often a crucial father figure in the brutal controversy over occupied territories and Israeli-Palestinian discord. Right-wing religious maximalist (e.g. Gush Emunim) justify their claims and cite the promises to the fathers, (esp. 12:7 "I will give this land to your offspring"; 13:15 "...for I will give all the land that you see to you and your offspring forever."; 15:18 On that day the Lord made a covenant with Abram, saying, "To your offspring I give this land from the river of Egypt to the great river, the river Euphrates"; 17:8 "I give the land you sojourn in to you and your offspring to come, all the land of Canaan, as an everlasting possession. I will be their God."; 22:17 "...your descendants shall seize the gates of their foes.") In these promises, religious expansionists find an **unconditional** right to the entire land of Palestine, if not beyond; while the rights of the local indigenous inhabitants are implicitly compared to the ancient Canaanites, who will either accept subservience or be wiped out.

Religious advocates of peace and territorial compromise look to Abraham no less. They cite Abraham's encounter with the Lord over the fate of Sodom to prove that in fact the right to the Promised Land is **conditional upon moral behavior of his descendants:** "For I have singled him out, that he may instruct his children and his posterity to keep the way of the Lord by doing what is right and just, In order that the Lord may bring about for Abraham what He has promised him" (18:19).

Moreover, Abraham's relations with local inhabitants over and over exemplify the way of the "paths of peace". He consistently avoids overt conflict or bloodshed, using strategies of territorial compromise with Lot to avert an incipient clash; respecting local authority (Melchizedek, Avimelech, Ephron) entering into peace treaties with Avimelech (and possibly Melchizedek) showing deference and restraint in dealing either with King of Sodom or Hittites and finally buying a burial plot in a legal contract, sold at the going merchant's rate.

Abraham's way of peace clashes dramatically with the massacre of inhabitants of Schechem by his great-grandchildren Shimeon and Levi. The possibility of successful peace treaties still existed during the period of Conquest, while during the Solomonic United Kingdom local autochthonous groups were treated as slaves, or indentured laborers. Through all this, Abraham remains, despite differing images of El Khalil/Father of Faith/ "Avraham Avinu", a figure of reconciliation. Within the protracted bloody struggle over this oft-promised land, the common father Abraham, remains a role model (and mentor) for one who did come to the land as a stranger but found ways to live peacefully with his neighbors and so once again give truth to the prophecy "And all the families of the earth shall bless themselves by you." (12:3).*

---

* Clash between contemporary religious interpretations of Abraham and the right to Land reflects a controversy between two of the most influential medieval biblical commentators Rashi and Ramban. Rashi cites Genesis 1 to show that all the land on earth belongs to the Lord who may it assign it unconditionally as He wishes; while Ramban, citing texts concerning Sabbatical Year or Lev 25-26 (...for the land belongs to me you are only strangers and guests (Lev.25:23); Deut. 28:58-68 "If you do not keep and observe all the words of this Law...you will be torn from the land...", argues strongly that residence and possession in the Land belongs to the Lord but is conditional on a maintained level of behavior moral- ethical-social superior to those of the original inhabitants.

Psalm of the Jealous God[70]

Who says
the Old Man
stayed his hand?
Are not his sons still slaughtered under the psalm
of the jealous god?

The pillars
have become markers,
the hand bears the name
of the slain
the stone dagger glitters
in the tear light,
and the stars
still remain
uncounted.

APPENDIX

The Common Cultural-ecological Background
Of The Patriarchs

In this appendix I discuss some of the common life-history, cultural and ecological characteristics of "Patriarchal Culture" (cf. De Vaux 1987; Mazar 1969; Albright 1961; Parrot 1962; Yeivin 1963; Woolley 1936; Sarna 1966; Speiser 1964; Pritchard 1969; Hallo & Simpson 1971; Livingston 1987; and more critically Thompson 1974; van Seters 1975). Whatever the origins of the "doublets and triplets" of Genesis, those stories which are repeated for the reader by the redactor, they present a consistent unified view of a common culture. The repetitions reflect a shared cultural repetoire of the Patriarchs as migrant, resident aliens forced to live by their wits. Such an evocation of a shared cultural repetoire is seen clearly in Abraham's problematic defense of his tricking Avimelech King of Gerar, (by calling himself brother, not husband of Sara). When asked, "What, then, was your purpose in doing this thing?" He replied:

> *I thought, surely there is no fear of God in this place, and they will kill me because of my wife, And besides, she is in truth my sister, my father's daughter though not my mother's; and she became my wife. So when God made me wander from my father's house I said to her, "Let this be a kindness that you shall do me: whatever place we come to, say of me: He is my brother."* (20:11-13).

Whatever else Abraham is doing (and surely saying he told only a "half truth" cannot "excuse" his behavior) he is stating that switching wife/sister is a part of his migrant-wanderer culture, a tradition which he passes onto his son (26:6-11).

In the text as we have it (i.e. the redacted text), there is a latent and an overt source of the repetitions and parallelisms. The latent or hidden parallels relate to the literary structure of the text, which was discussed above in terms of "chiastic parallelism". But this parallelism is implicit, and despite generations of Biblical scholarship, only recently re-discovered. The overt reason for the parallels, I suggest is the "culture concept". Genesis describes a "family history" (in which God almost seems another member of the family) who share the same dilemmas and cultural repetoire or heritage with which to respond to these social, political, ecological and spiritual challenges. Although we may never be able to know fully how Biblical events are related to cultural artifacts available to us from the ancient Near East or contemporary ethnography, we may describe Abraham's culture in its own terms, using the text, as one might use an old ethnographic report. In this way, we may provide a social and cultural backdrop for Abraham's life history.

Geography and Spiritual Climate of the Holy Land

The action of Genesis spans the entire Fertile Crescent, that semi-circle of arable land surrounding the Syrian desert (De Vaux 1978). Canaan is in the southernmost third of the descending part and is the least fertile section of the crescent. The land of the Bible is divided in four distinct regions (coastal plain, inland valleys, central hill country, rift valley). The patriarchs are almost exclusively restricted to the central hill country and the southern (Negev) desert, i.e. they seem to have avoided the major centers of population along the coast and in the rich alluvial valleys. This country has extreme and unpredictable weather conditions based on a California-like wet winter/dry summer rainfall pattern. Snow is not unknown.

Like Greece, Canaan lacks geographical unity. Its sharp contours, differences in soil and climate, lead to a patchwork of small ecological niches, each with its own way of life which in turn tend to crystallize and consolidate a local tribal identity. The political structure which Abraham and his sons encounter is one of weak central authority, independent city states or elders with local kings, who may grant residency rights.

Historically, according to De Vaux 1978 and others, Palestine may flourish as in an integrated powerful independent political force only when the regional Great Powers, such as Egypt, or Babylon, are in decline. The local isolation contrasts with the geographical and strategic importance of Canaan as a land bridge between Africa and Asia, between the Mediterranean and Middle East.

All the sites where patriarchs stopped - Haran, Schechem, Bethel, Hebron - located along the central hill country in a region with 10-20 inches of rain per year, "on the average" but with great yearly variation. This is is an ecological niche suited for grazing animals bordering on the fringe of the desert, in contact but separate from the agricultural - based towns in the plain i.e. between the desert and the sown.

The patriarchs were not true nomads as they were not sedentary but probably "dimorphous" semi-nomads on the move, Abraham seems always wandering, perhaps tended to a settled life as an expedient. The land itself lacks natural resources and the contrast "between the poverty of the natural resources" has led a number of commentatators, to note the contrast with the "greatest of its spiritual destiny". There is somehow a suggestion that an ethical monotheism could only emerge in a harsh land without luxury within the framework of the extended family to develop deep personal relationships and so discover truely human values (De Vaux 1978).

Shared Cultural and Life History Patterns

From the point of view of the "stories themselves", all the patriarchs faced a common set of physical and social pressures. Each dealt with similar geographic, ecological, socio-economic and ethnic conditions. Each in turn responded to these challenges using their shared cultural heritage, as crafty but marginal pastoralist.

The major elements of their cultural heritage appear to be: mobility, marginality, endogamy and kin solidarity; use of craftiness, even deceit and disguise, especially toward local authority; inheritance not by first born (primogeniture) but by last born (ultimatogeniture); and theophany - the direct revelation by divinity

The ecological challenges they faced seem to be thoses of marginal semi-nomads, herders of sheep and goat not attached to one spot. In addition to seasonal moves in search of fresh pasture and water sources, each of the "fathers" undertook a great migration or wished to do so. (Isaac was forbidden to "go down to Egypt" (26:2)).

Marginal men on the move have serious limits on their material culture. Everything they owned has to be transportable; their possession and their "God" had to be able to move with them, not, as in the case of Babylonian or Cannanite Temple gods, fixed in one location. Moreover, herding often requires long periods of isolation and solitude - a prerequisite for the cycle of withdrawal and return of the life pattern of spiritual revolutionaries.

The challenges each family faced seem all of a piece. Within the family, there is the curse of infertility with the use of handmaidens as "surrogate mothers" (with more success in the case of Jacob and less in the case of Abraham). Prayer intercession was also a device used by Abraham (for the women of Gerar) and by Isaac (for his own wife), as well as other fertility magic e.g. mandrakes. (30:14f).

The outer challenge was finding a place to live, to survive as a stranger without rights, to live mostly by one's wits, relying heavily on one's blood relatives (yet cf. 14:13-24; 21:22-32 for relations with non-relatives). Famine and inconsistent rainfall are common occurences in Canaan; each man sought solutions to this key dilemma. Egypt held a great attraction with its consistent source of water; local conflicts over water rights and digging new wells were also common (21:25-30; 26:18-33).

Parallel cousin marriage reinforced the emphasis on close kin cooperation. Abram made his wife his sister; Jacob married wives who were sisters; Isaac had an arranged marriage with a paternal cousin, his father's brother's grandaughter.

To pastoralists, cities are centers of evil, and distrust of authorities is the only sensible policy. All the fathers were willing to show deference to locals when the situation demanded it, as Abraham's purchase of the burial cave, Isaac's peace treaty and the false pact of Jacob at Schechem reveal. They did use strategems illustrating need for self reliance, compelled like tricksters to live by their wits.

Societies differ greatly in the degree of stigma associated with infertility and the degree to which they offer culturally acceptable alternatives. Contemporary career oriented society in the United States is a society which places relatively less importance on having children of one's own - indeed delayed reproduction, (putting off having kids:) or declined paternity maternity ("deciding not to have kids at all") are socially accepted attitudes. America, therefore is an example of a "youth-oriented" but not "child-oriented" society. Most cultures place a premium on having biological children and continue to do so despite the best intended family planning programs - since children are the most reliable guarantee of economic security and "symbolic immortality"; the continuity of me, my name, my family, my people, my life...

Contemporary Israeli society, in contrast, places a great emphasis on children (child-oriented culture) and reproduction. "So why don't you have children, already?" is a question strangers readily ask young couples on the bus. An indication of the cultural difference in attitudes toward infertility is an Israeli adaptation of "life events: social readjustment rating scale". It asked Israelis to rate which events would require the greatest readjustment.

"Found out cannot have children" was fourth most stressful, ahead of death of parent, a war, divorce or being in a bus when a bomb went off.

Of the three more stressful events, the first two most stressful events were likewise child related: "Lost son in military action" and "Child dies". The third, "Death of a Spouse", was the most stressful in American version. Infertility, surprisingly, does not even appear in the American original! (Levav et. al 1981)

Cultures vary in providing alternatives in the case of chronic infertility. In the United States, a broad range of options exist: adoption, insemination, artificial fertilization etc. even "surrogate motherhood." Abraham's culture did offer a special form of surrogate mother via a wife's handmaiden. Indeed some legal contracts from the ancient Near East specify it under certain conditions (De Vaux 1978), e.g. for certain "priestesses" ("naditu") who were not allowed to bear children (Teubel 1984); or in case of infertility. "Surrogate motherhood" must be distinguished from polygamy, in which one man has more than one wife. Polygamy is another strategy to avoid infertility and increase a man's (but not woman's) reproductive capacity. "Surrogate motherhood" is a special form of natal adoption ("perhaps I shall have a son through her" lit. "be built up" with worth, a play on "ben", "son" and: "banah", "build up" (JPS note p.23). Other techniques mentioned in Genesis include prayer ("Isaac pleaded with the Lord on behalf of his wife" 25:21), herbal medicine or magic (30:14-15), surgery (17:11) and probably pilgrimage to sacred sites (Abramovitch & Bilu 1986).

Common Life History Patterns

In addition to a common cultural tradition, the fathers shared certain life history patterns. We know little about their childhood, but often much about the conditions surrounding their conception, birth and naming. Each was separated as an adult from their father and was forced to discover for himself a life of self-reliance. Each experienced the death or traumatic separation of an elder brother - the death of Abraham's brother, the banishment of Ishmael, the flight from Esau, and partly as a result each experienced periods of isolation, often under life threatening circumstances.

Famine, as we noted played a central role and often caused further migration and desperate acts to preserve of self preservation. Abram and his grandson both visited Egypt and Mesopotamia, the two great civilizations and one infers that exposure to these great traditions must have had an important impact on their spiritual devlopment. Famine in turn is based on water as The Scarce Resource. There is evidence that new wells were dug but that this in turn led to conflicts over water rights with the local inhabitants. Under favorable conditions treaties were "cut" with the local king. Note too that well is a place where couples first meet, marriages arranged and hospitality offered. Wells also function as important spiritual locations e.g. Well of the Seeing God for Hagar, Ishmael and Isaac.

There is a strong emphasis on endogamy, marrying close kin such as paternal parallel cousins and a corresponding rejection of locals as potential kin i.e. refusal to enter into wife exchange. There is, nevertheless, a pattern of conflict with the primary wife, initially over fertility and ultimately over inheritance. Relations with sons are troubled but reconciliation is finally achieved in old age of the father. All live to see grandchildren and are buried in the cave at Hebron, the family sepulchre.

Each has a personal revelation of the Divine in dreams, trances and other theophanies. Their God is identified to the sons as the "God of Abraham" who reconfers the blessings. In practice, there is a cycle of promise, the apparent disconfirmation of the promises and their ultimate reconfirmation and realization. The process is also seen in that each acquires a divinely appointed name (Isaac before birth) in which the semantics of the given etymology exemplifies the new destiny and sense of rebirth.

Thus the patriarchs shared the same basic life concerns. They sought assurance for the continuation of their clan and their name after them; an intimate relation to the God of Abraham, in the land that was promised to him; including political security in the land which they inheirted only symbolically and finally, they shared a desperate need to become fathers not only to their own sons but also to the nations who would derive from their loins.

"The Name of God"

According to the priestly account of the call of Moses (Exod. 6:3 6:4), "El Shaddai" was the name of the God of Abraham, Isaac and Jacob. Also according to the priestly account, God revealed himself to Abraham as "El Shaddai" (17:1). (De Vaux 1978:276). De Vaux also argues that originally the god of the father was **anonymous**, which is consistent with the Yaweh tradition of Gen 15, in which he reveals his Divine Name:
"I am the Lord who brought you out of Ur of the Chaldees" (15:7). In the Hebrew text, what is translated as "Lord" is the tetragrammaton "YHWH" יהוה conventionally but incorrectly vocalized as Jahweh (Jews never attempt to vocalized the tetragammaton but use the word "Adonei", which is accurately translated as "Lord"; in non-religious contexts, the euphemism השם "hashem", "the Name (of God)" is used. Older traditions in Talmud etc. do speak of vocalizing tradition, which were secret, restricted to high Priests and carried magical powers.)
      In the following verse (v.8), when Abram addresses Jahweh/YHWH, he actually calls his "adonei Jahweh" i.e, "Lord God" but might be better translated "My Lord Yahweh" (Jerusalem Bible 1968).
      What is the relation of Yahweh/YHWH to El Elyon? The situation is complicated by the term "El Elyon" which occurs only in the incident involving Melchizedek (Gen. 14), and, in Ps. 78:35 ("...remembering that God was their rock, God Most High (el elyon), their redeemer.") Used alone with el, the word elyon, "most high", is common in the rest of the Bible as a title or substitute for Yahweh. "There is no evidence anywhere for El Elyon outside the Bible. In fact, El and Elyon are two different deities in the Canaanite-Phoenician patheon and were arbitrarily combined in Gen. 14" (De Vaux 1978:275). "El was the highest God in the Canaanite pantheon. At Ugarit, he was called father of the gods and "creator of creatures". This "creation", however, was a procreation, since El procreated rather than created. In one text, El is described copulating with two women in order to procreate the gods... he was given the title of Bull, which clearly shows him as powerful rather than as begetter... He was the ideal king and he presided over the assembly of the gods in his palace, ... wise and kind, showing sadness and happiness, but never anger. The Canaanite religion of El was very different from the religion of the god of the father. It was above all the religion of a settled people - El was the head of a pantheon, a king living in a palace and surrounded by a court of other gods, the master of the world who never intervened in human history.
      In assimilating El into the religion of the god of the father, the ancestors of Israel in no sense abandoned their nomadic religion, but rather enriched it... as the

all-powerful cosmic god, enlarging the idea of God to include the whole world, rather than simply the family or clan. (de Vaux 1978: 282). Or to put it more succinctly, De Vaux argues that "the god of the father became assimilated to the great god El." (op.cit. 456).

Patriarchal Religion

In terms of religious practices, the patriarchs erected altars (12:7; 12:8; 13:18; 26:25; 33:20; 35:7) and offered animal sacrifices - although we are not told what or how they made offerings. Ironically, the only sacrifice described in detail is the substitute offering of the ram in Gen. 22 as an "olah", or whole burnt offering. There was no fixed place for sacrifice or fixed sanctuary; God could be addressed everywhere.

Abraham is associated with special trees, and just prior to the akeda plants a tree and calls upon the name of the Lord "el olam", "Everlasting God". Such a possibly "sacred tree" was a practice anathema to later times (Deut. 16:21: Ex. 34:13; Deut. 12:3) and Jacob's dealing with "mazzeboth" (like Rachel's desire for "teraphim") are likewise subsequently condemned (Ex. 23:23; 34:13; Deut. 7:7; 12:3).

The major religious innovation which initiates the patriarchal era is the introduction of circumcision at the earliest life cycle ritual. For Abraham, Ishmael and the rest of the males of the camp, circumcision was a group adult ritual, symbolizing the collective unity of Abraham's camp. It embraced the new covenant with God, under a new name, El Shaddai, for Ishmael, as it remains for many Moslems, an initiation separating boyhood from manhood (cf. cryptic Ex. 4:25). But for Isaac, circumcision is an individual initiation by the father of his infant son into the covenant, a pre-conscious male-spiritual initiation.

"The most important aspect of the religion of the patriarchs is the cult of "god of the father" (De Vaux 1978: 268). "From the moment that he became the head of a family, Abraham had the right to choose his own god. And the chosen god then became a part of the family, serving in fact as its real head." (Gonzalez 1967:19). The irony and basis for the spiritual revolutionary is the God of Abraham was not the god of **his** father, but a new God; at first apparently nameless, He became for his sons and grandsons and descendants ever after, God of the Fathers.

"The chosen God of Abraham could have been either accepted or rejected by Abraham's sons" (Gonzalez 1967:19). This dilemma, we shall argue, is part of the crux in the later psychology of the spiritual revolutionary in the period of institutionalizing his breakthrough. If son-disciple is allowed to reject the God of his Father just as Abraham did, then the spiritual innovation will be for nothing. A flash in the spiritual pan. A momentary diversion instead of an everlasting line. Thus the son-as-disciple is both the son-of-promise, and the threat to that very same promise. The son, unknowingly is the greatest danger to his father as a spiritual revolutionary. For Abraham, the dilemma was how to ensure that his God, the God of Abraham, will be the God for Isaac and hence, the God of my Father[18].

Religion of Abraham vs. Religion of Moses

Abraham's faith, as we have seen, was a religion for men on the move. The head of the family was also priest and prophet. Abraham's theophanies and sacrifices were not limited to any single place or fixed ritual. The religion of Moses, as it evolved from Sinai until the Jerusalem Temple, reflects a transition from tribal equality of pastoral life to settled hierarchy of centralized state and agriculture. Formal contact with the divine became limited to official sacrifices, mediated by a hereditary priest caste. Moses introduced a formal legal code and strict punishment, including ostracism or execution for offenders. In contrast Abraham was given only the commandment of circumcision and there is no account of how he dealt with sinners or wrongdoers. His general tenor is that of seeking compromise. Moses is thus the impassioned particularistic national leader while Abraham, the tribal chief, exhibits a universal ethical attitude.

NOTES

1. cf. Ross 1982; Shapiro (1984:71): "We have a new term now to describe the character of the abandoning or infanticidal father, 'the Laius complex'. It is a term that developed when psychotherapists realized that Freud had skewed the Oedipus story; the myth is not simply about a regicidal and incestuous son but also about an infanticidal father. Laius orders his son put to death. In fact, Sophocles' great drama, Oedipus Rex, is about our capacity to see 'all' the violence in families, not just one side of it.

    The Bible, too, may be read as a struggle to make men more responsible as fathers - less infanticidal, more aware of their jealousy, more willing to consider the claims of 'all' their children. One of the Bible's basic themes is paternity. God is the father who cares, and men are commanded to be more like him. God teaches men to be protective toward members of their immediate children of God. This jealous God values fidelity and loyalty. He is molding a new kind of family, one that is bonded not only by property but also by care, patriarchal but not infanticidal. This God needs the help of men, who often rebel against the tasks of manhood, especially against being compassionate fathers.

    Infanticidal envy continues to afflict fathers. Many fathers are unable to overcome the envy they harbor for the son in the womb or for the son sucking at the breast. The child's first task is often to survive his father's envy - by smiling, by hiding, by any means possible. Moses, Jesus and Oedipus all narrowly survive infanticidal rage."

    Significantly, Hebrew midrash describes the infant Abraham threatened by King Nimrod in a manner akin to Moses, Jesus and Oedipus - escaping only by hiding alone in a cave - where his own fingers gave him suck and nourishment. In Erich Neumann's schema of the History and Origins of Consciousness, this stage is "the uruboros" (Neumann 1954). In terms of Abraham's Laius complex, the Akeda would be the "ritual psychodrama" resolving once and for **all** the "temptation" of infanticidal envy.

    In a family dynamic perspective (Boszormenyi-Nagy and Krasner 1986), the reaction of a father with a Laius complex is that of a childhood victim, turned victimizer, an inheritance which is in turn passed on to his son - who in turn, unconsciously or preconsciously, victimizes his own children. Such a dynamic is made all the more vicious when narcisstic elements, such as "destructive entitlement" preclude the possibility of mutual empathy and the rediscovery of "trustworthiness". In such cases, the emotional pain of the victimizer as victim is so great, he is not able to see and empathize with his victim's pain. Contextual Family Therapy of Boszormenyi-Nagy argues that first the father-victimizer must be given recognition as a victim in order to break the intergenerational cycle of family violence and mistrust. A fuller discussion of the family dynamics approach to Genesis is beyond the scope of this work but would be a fruitful approach to such family problems as sibling rivalry brought on by paternal preference, the theme of fratricide, fertility, disguise, etc.

2.   cf.Gros Louis (1982:74-5): "Surely as readers of a literary narrative, we must keep in mind the previous history detailed in Genesis 12-19 as we read Chapter 22. We may not know where the Lord speaks from, but we do know that he has spoken to Abraham before; we may not know where Abraham is or what he is doing when he answers "Here I am", but we do know that he has answered the Lord before,.. What Abraham does in chapter 22 is not an existential act, but part of a coherent continuum that is not obscure to us as readers; indeed, given what has gone before in the narrative, what he does seems less a climatic moment and more like a coda, a final refrain that recalls for us the themes of Abraham's life and epitomizes them in a highly compressed scene, the tone of which is quiet, direct, simple." Likewise, Rosenberg (1986:83): "...Gen. 22 sweeps up into its vortex virtually every major theme and motif set forth in the preceding ten chapters. During the few, swift strokes of its progression, it momentarily 'represents' the cycle, refracting it in an enigmatic and nightmarish inversion. The fuller import of this strategem can only be seen when we explore the cycle's relation to the rest of Genesis, and to related texts outside of Genesis."

3.   I treat the text of Genesis 12-25 not as myth, folklore, nor as composite of various sources, form, or traditions. In a way, I adopt a naive view to take the text as it appears, the history of a life or a "life history" (Watson 1976; White 1952, 1964; Langness & Frank 1981; Allport 1942; Buhler 1935, 1968; Butler 1968; Crapanzano 1977, 1980; Dollard 1935; Erikson 1975; Frenkel 1936) There are hints of "life history" approach to in Rabbinic comments, such as the one claiming that King Solomon wrote Song of Songs in his youth, Proverbs in Middle Age and Ecclesisteses in old age. Aside from the thorny question of whether these three works might have been written by a single individual, this Rabbinic comment highlights the different "Seasons of a Man's Life" (Levinson 1978), in the life cycle (Erikson 1963). Thus Song of Songs illustrates the

passions of youth and the search for intimacy/isolation which Erikson emphasizes in young adulthood. Proverbs, with its concern to advise the coming generation ("Listen, my sons, to your father's instruction... 1.8) describes the search for generativity and fear of stagnation ("all who hate me are in love with death" 8;36; "A foolish son is his father's sorrow and the grief of her who gave him birth" 17:25;) while Ecclesiastes is an account of an old man's struggle to main ego integrity in the face of ego despair. The same phases of early, mid and late adulthood are apparent in the stories of David, Jacob and Moses. cf.Friedman (1987) "Who Wrote the Bible?" for a very readable recent version concerning authorship issues.

4. For recent contributions of computer assisted statistical lingustics to issue of authorship in Genesis, cf. Radday et.al. (1985) or Wenham (1988), who argue that there is no "discernable difference" between J and E. Narrative material is distinct from human or divine speech; the language of the primeval sage (1-11) is very distinct from the rest of Genesis, and there is some contrast between Abraham/Jacob stories (12-36) and the Joseph story (37-50).
Genesis 14 is associated with J narrative, though standard source criticism regards this chapter as an isolated boulder. Many of these conclusions, however, have been anticipated by recent work of Westermann 1981; Coats 1983; Vawter 1977; Alexander 1982.

5. Literally, "generation, generation, and its interpretors" as in many proverbs, there is a verbal play with "dor" and "dorshav". cf. Silver (1982:ix-xi): "I have long been of the opinion that the continuities within any religious tradition are formal and institutional rather than doctrinal. Words are empty vessels into which successive generations of believers pour the wine of their convictions...Believers forget that though they read from an old scripture and feel bound to its institutions, they inevitably read into it their feelings and needs and shape its instructions to fit current perceptions of what is right and proper... The tendency to change derives from a basic need for reassurance. Life is brief. Our experiences are confusing. Much of what constitutes religion satisfies the human need to create a sense of order and stability in the midst of flux...the religious heroes of the past, like the concepts and ceremonies consecrated in Scripture, become vessels into which a tradition pours new values and ideas as they come to seem appropriate."

6. Midrash did invent a childhood for Abraham, the most famous legend is the story of the "breaking of the idols": Terah, Abram's father was a maker of idols, statues of the gods. Left alone in his father's workshop, Abram takes a

hammer and smashes all the idols except the largest in whose hand he places
the hammer. Terah, on discovering the terrible scene of his gods destroyed,
demands an explanation and is told that the gods quarelled among themselves
about who was strongest until they smashed each other to bits. cf. Bereshit
Rabba 37:19; Qu'ran Sura 21 : 52-59; Box (1904) Appendix to Apocalypse of
Abraham in which he compares various versions, and Wildavksy (1984:244,
n.33): "It took several readings to convince me that childhood memories of
Abram as a boy smashing the idols in his father's house were legends not
included in the Bible."
There are hardly any legends about Abram's mother except to note her absence,
as a well-known tale of him being suckled by his own finger in a cave. Such a
legend points to theme of "self creation"; just as the idol smashing reveals his
intelligence and youthful rebellion in which he takes moral responsibility for
his father (cf. Erikson (1969) and his analysis Gandhi's relation to his dying
father). It also indirectly shows how much "God-making" was part of the
family business.

7. The additions include a praise poem recited by the Egyptians to pharaoh about
Sarai's charm and beauty and an elaboration of the night Abram spent on the
border of Egypt prior to "crossing over". The text tells of a dream of Abram's
in which he dreamed of a cedar and a date palm standing side by side. Men
come to cut down and uproot the cedar tree but are persuaded not to do so on
account of the date palm. Abram interprets the masculine-feminine symbolism
of cedar versus date palm as referring to himself and Sarai. On the basis of the
dream, Abram then says: "I am well aware that you are a beautiful woman. If
the Egyptians see you and think, 'She is my wife' they will kill me and let you
live. Say that you are my sister, that it may go well with me because of you;
and that I may remain alive thanks to you" (12:12-13).

cf.Pritchard (1969) for Sumerian fables based on the conflict of a cedar and a
date palm.

8. For a discussion of "word play" and other literary features of the Hebrew text,
cf. Preminger & Greenstein 1986; Fokkelman, in Alter & Kermode (1987) ;
Alter 1981, 1985; Sternberg 1985).

9. For a discussion of the difficulties and decisions in translating the Hebrew
Bible cf. Speiser 1964; Orlinsky 1966; Greenstein 1983; Glassman 1981; and
Walter Benjamin's seminal essay "The Task of the The Translator" (1969).
Perhaps the most interesting attempt to bridge the gap between author and

audience oriented translation was the German Buber-Rosenzweig translation, which did try to convey the original "breath groups" and "Leitwort": "by translating Hebrew words according to the sense of the stem to allow the repetition of various words built on the same root appear to the audience". Cf. E. Fox, (1971; 1972) for a discussion of Buber-Rosenzweig approach to translation (E. Fox, "We Mean the Voice: The Buber-Rosenzweig Translation of the Bible" Response 12 (Winter 1971-1972); and "In the Beginning: An English Rendition of the Book of Genesis" Response 14 (Summer 1972).
See also Livingston (1987:63): "The Hebrew verb system differs from that found in Indo-European systems. Hebrew verbs are not based on tense and mood. The time element must be gained mostly from context. Instead, the Hebrew verb stresses completed action, incomplete action, continuous action, intensive action or caused action. Its conjugation differs from that in English for example. There is a strong emotional element in the average Hebrew verb and in many nouns. This emotional tone is often completely lost in translation into English." For a comprehensive overview written from a Christian perspective, see Jon deWaard and Eugene Nida (1986).

10. Dahlberg (1982) discusses these and other themes in his essay "The Unity of Genesis" e.g.... "A correspondence exists between the beginning and ending stories in Genesis. The serpent had declared, "You will be like God..." Joseph exclaims, 'Am I in the Place of God?' The serpent had promised, "... knowing good and evil." Joseph declares, "You meant evil against me, but God meant it for good." The serpent had said, "You will not die..." Joseph perceives life saved from death: "God meant...to bring it about that many people should be kept alive as they are today." It seems that the use of these specific words in Joseph's conversation with his brothers, a conversation in which he in effect responds to the serpent's lines (3:4-5) point for point, serves and is intended to serve dramatically and theologically of the scene portrayed earlier in Eden, and as a problem exposed there. (Dahlberg (1982:129). See also Forsyth (1991).

11. Rendsburg (1986:27-52) analyzes the chiastic structure of the main body of the Abraham narrative (11:27-22:24):

A: Geneology of Terah (11:27-32)
B: Start of Abram's Spiritual Odyssey (12:1-9)
C: Sarai in foreign palace; ordeal ends in peace & success, Abram and Lot part (12:10-13:18)
D: Abram comes to the rescue of Sodom and Lot (14:1-24)
E: Covenant with Abram; Annuciation of Ishmael (15:1-16:16)

E': Covenant with Abraham; Annuciation of Isaac (17:1-18:15)
D': Abraham comes to the rescue of Sodom and Lot (18:16, 19:38)
C': Sarah in foreign palace; ordeal ends in peace & success; Abraham and Ishmael part (20:1-21:34)
B': Climax of Abraham's Spiritual Odyssey (22:1-19)
A': Geneology of Nahor (22:20-24)

Moreover, he argues that the "linking material" 23:1-25:18 almost parallels later "linking material" of 35:23-36:43, as follows;

A: Death and burial of Sarah (23:1-20)
B: Marriage of Isaac (24:1-67)
C: Abraham's sons (25:1-6)
D: Death and burial of Abraham (25:7-11)
E: Ishmael's sons (25:12-18)

A': o
B': Marriage of Esau (36:1-5)
C': Jacob's sons (35:23-26)
D': Death and Burial of Isaac (35:27-29)
E': Esau's sons (36:6-43)

The absence of a parallel for A: Death and burial of Sarah, highlights the absence of any account of the death and burial of Rebekah, "one of Genesis' most glaring lacunas" (Rendsburg 1986:72). Rebekah presumably died while her beloved son, Jacob, was absent in Haran, possibly as a result of the curse which she took upon herself: "Your curse, my son, be upon me" (27:13).

Key vocabulary items link not only parallel units but also link successive units as well, Rensburg argues that such a verbal repetition help clear up many puzzling aspects of the text, such as the connection between 14:22 and 19:23-4, as both use or evoke the phrase "heaven and earth".

In the main body parallelsim, there is no counterpart for the birth, circumcision and rearing of Isaac, but in patriarchal narratives, births are given little attention, while annuciations are dominant (16:7-14; 18:9-15; 25:21-23). Likewise, Rensburg shows that the internal parallelism of C/C'is not exact (Ca Cb Cc/C'a C'c C'b) to make two passages dealing with opening the womb contiguous and allow for the passage of time between Isaac the infant and Isaac the grown lad.

NOTES 155

Rosenberg analyzes the chiastic structure as follows:

a   Geneological framework (11:10-25,26-32)
b   Migration from Haran; separation from Nahor (12:4-5)
c   Building of altars; land promised (12:4-9; (13:14-18))
d   "Wife-sister" episode (12:10-20)
e   Border agreement with Lot (13:1-13)
f   Sodom episode and rescue of Lot (14:1-24)
g   Covenant of sacrifice (15:1-20)

X   Expulsion and Rescue of Hagar

g': Covenant of circumcision (17:1-27)
f': Sodom episode and rescue of Lot (18:1-19:38)
e': Border agreement with Abimelech (21:22-34)
d': "Wife-sister" episode (20:1-18)
c': Building of altar (22:6); land promised (17b); acquired (23:1-20)
b': Migration to Haran; unification with Nahor (24:1-67)
a': Geneological framework ((22:20-24) ; 25:1-18)

The main differences between Rosenberg 1986:84 "(nearly) symmetrical component of the Cycle" and Rensburg is that Rosenberg sees the narrative pivot on the Expulsion and rescue of Lot; and he tries to incorporate 23:1-25:18 in the same parallelism, while Rensburg analyzes this "linking material" separately. Aside from these (and a few other minor details) both versions are essentially in agreement that "the second half of the cycle expands, deepens, and sometimes twists and overturns the meaning of the thematic elements set forth in the first... the second half represent both traditionary 'variations' and narrative 'developments' of their predecessors in the first...the Akeda story supplies a chilling reversal of expectations generated throughout virtually the whole cycle." (Rosenberg 1986:82-3), Rosenberg also argues that the narrative is based on a geographical parallelism balancing east/west and north/south; and the two Hagar stories chapter 16 and 21 together are parallels of the Akeda (22:1-19).

He also notes fascinating parallels between Abraham and Sarah with the Garden story and ahead to the future patriarchs: Abraham, like the first human beings, begins his active career repudiating the kin of his place of origin (Gen 2:18-24/12:1ff), and ends it by resuming his tie with his ancestral lineage (3:19-21/42:1ff). If we extend the borders of the Garden story into Gen. 4 we find that each patriarch in Genesis recapitulates the major lines of the primordial story: experiences radical severance from kin; experiences collaboration and scandal with a closely kindred wife; acquiesces in the advancement of one child over another; witnesses the exile of a child; and experiences a first taste of mortality through the presumed death of a child. (Rosenberg 1986:96).

12. Contrast Morgenstern (1965:188): "The various stories are but loosely connected. Almost any one, with the possible exceptions of the call of Abraham and the sacrifice of Isaac, might have been omitted without having seriously impaired the unity of the Abraham story as a whole, and without our being conscious that anything was lacking."

Concerning the similarity cf. Sarna 1966:161-2:

In Haran, God had introduced His call by the words, "Go forth...to the land that I will show you" (12:1). At the akeda, God employed similar language, "Go forth...to the land of Moriah...on one of the heights which I will point out to you" (22:2). Just as previously the exact destination was withheld, so here the patriarch was not initially to know the terminal point of his journey. As in the one case, the tension of the drama about to be enacted is heightened by the accumulation of descriptive epithets - "your land, your homeland, your father's house" - so in the latter case, the same effect is created by the employment of the identical device, - "your son, your favored one, Isaac, whom you love." In Haran, son took leave of father forever; at Akeda, father and son were prepared to see each other for the last time. Having obediently fulfilled his first mission, the patriarch found himself faced with a situation of grave danger to Sarah, followed by defections from the family circle. The identical pattern of events recurs this time, but prior to receiving the last mission, Sarah is in great peril and Abraham's kith and kin are sent away. The divine order to journey forth having been completed, Abraham built an altar at the "terebinth of Moreh". So at the end of his final ordeal, the patriarch brought an offering on the altar he had built on one of the heights of Moriah. Finally the two narratives share in common divine blessings that are strikingly similar in content.

The Torah, then, has used the ancient Akeda tale to encase the account of the spiritual odyssey of Abraham within a literary framework, opening and closing with divine communications that involve agonizing decisions carried to completion with unflinching loyalty, and culminating in promises of a glorious posterity."
cf. also Gros Louis (1982:80-1): "The journey to Moriah is a microcosm of

Abraham's longer journey, which began when he immediately obeyed the Lord's command that he leave his country, his kindred and his father's house (indeed, the very language of 22:2 echoes that of Genesis 12:1-2)";
Greenwood (1981:125): "To appreciate the semiotic significance of the sacrificial mandate, one should see it in relation to the denotative content of the promise made in Genesis 12:1-3. The sacrifical mandate and the previous promise might seem to stand in striking contradiction to each other...";
Rouiller (1978:17): "...and go": this expression is already found in 12:1. Moreover, stylistically these two verses have a curious resemblance. In both cases we have a detailed description of what Abraham must leave land, home, father's house (12:1), only son, the one whom you love, Isaac (22:2). In both cases, there is a similarly undefined goal to attaint "Go...to the land that I will show you" (52:1); "go to the land...of which I shall tell you" 22:2). Are these similarities purely accidental? We believe rather that the Elohist did not wish to isolate the episode of Genesis 22 from the entire career of Abraham.

13. cf. "Old Age in Genesis" in Sternberg (1985:349-64).

14. cf. also Gould (1978); and Levinson (1968).

15. Although we are primarily concerned in Genesis as a personal document revealing the life history of the Patriarch, it cannot be denied that the stories also functioned and continue to function in other ways. Perhaps the most important was how the stories of the Patriarch served to guide or justify later historical events or controversies. Limiting ourselves to Abraham we find him as precursor, prefiguring the sorjourn in Egypt because of famine and in a literal way the Exodus and return to the promised land. He makes sacrifice at places which in later historical era were thought to be cult centers; He lays down a tradition for division of spoils of war (cf. I Sam. 30:25) but asks nothing for himself, the mark of the true leader.
In Gen. 15 he is given an explicit vision of Egyptian exile and return; Gen. 14 he gives recognition to priest King and gives him 10%, coinciding with the later-day tithing at Jerusalem. Circumsion is said to begin with Abraham, which remains, in infant form, the lasting mark of his descendants. Birth of a promised son after long period of female infertility is another recurrent theme in the Bible. The sacrifice at Mt. Moriah is later identified with the Temple Mount (II Chr. 3:1) and possible other institutions connected with the period of the United Kingdom (David, Solomon) (Clements 1967) or later (van Seters 1975).

16. For further discussion of succession, cf. Goody, Succession to High Office, Cambridge University Press.

17. Talmon goes on to discuss the dilemma in Kibbutz life:

"The formation of families and the birth of children within the kibbutzim confronted the collective with the problem of internal family attachments... Family ties are based on an exclusivist and discriminating loyalty which sets the members of one's family more or less apart from others. Families may easily become competing.
The urge of the first settlers to immigrate to a new country and establish a kibbutz was the outcome of a kind of conversion that entailed a total change in outlook and way of life...The pioneering ideology appealed mainly to the young and unattached. It induced them to sever their relations with parents, to discard their former attachments, to disengage themselves totally from their social setting...Deep attachment to one's spouse and children based on purely affective interpersonal relations may gain precedence over the more ideological and more task-oriented relations with comrades." (op. cit.)

In the contemporary kibbutz, the conflict was resolved decisively in favor of family values, in what Max Weber called the "routinization of charisma". With the growth of larger private apartments, family sleeping arrangements and prosperity, there has been a switch from a "Gemeinschaft" group dynamics, instrument for Zionist and socialist revolution, ascetic, nature-oriented large ideo-emotional "family" to "Gesellschaft" of friendship and kinship, with consumption-orientation to material comforts, a production-oriented society comprised of separate biological families, striving for "self actualization", the achievement of personal ambition. (Krausz 1983).

18. The Samaritan version of the Pentateuch records that Terah lived only 145 years presumably to allow Abram to leave after his father's death (Vawter 1977:173); a tradition reflected in the New Testament during Stephen's speech to the Sanhedrin: "...after his father died, God made him leave Haran and come to this land where you are living today..." (Acts 7:3).

19. cf. van Rad (1976:158): "Strange that Milcah's father is named but not the father of the much more important Sarai!"

20. It is possible that, to the contrary, this Haran, father of Milcah and Iscah, is to be distinguished from Haran, Abram's brother.

21. Another well known Midrash expresses some of the theme of survivorship. Abram was cast by the local tyrant into a burning furnace but was not consumed. Haran, seeing Abram's salvation, impetuously rushed to join him and was consumed, burnt to death in the presence of his father, an idol worshiper. Another version tells of Haran rushing back to save gods from Terah's burning house. cf. Bereshit Rabba 37f.

22. cf.Parrot (1962); Sarna (1966); and Gordon (1955) who argues that this northern city was the Biblical Ur.

    Ur, Abram's native city (or perhaps city of his kindred - the Hebrew "moledet" from the root "yaledet" to give birth, to be born, may mean either or both) was one of the great cities of the ancient world, the "cradle of Sumerian civilization" (cf. Kramer 1950; Hallo and Simpson 1963; Wooley 1935: Pritchard 1969). The last great flourishing, Ur III dynasty was overrun by invaders in 1936 B.C.E. Since no firm date can be given to Abram (Thompson 1974; van Seters 1975; Thompson 1987), it is not possible to connect their migration with these or other known historical events. What is known is that the Chaldeans did not appear until 9th century B.C.E. and were not a power in southern Mesopotamia until somewhat later (van Seters 1975). The use of the term "Ur of the Chaldeans" was a gloss of the narrated to explain which city and perhaps to differentiate it from others e.g. Urfa, near Haran in Kurdistan border region. (cf. also Neh.9:7). The only other puzzle is that Ur and Haran in later Neo-Babylonian period, during the reign of Nabonidus, both had temples dedicated to "sin" (nanna), the moon god (van Seters 1975; Parrot 1962). Whether these traditions existed in Abram's time remains a tantalizing speculation. If so, then Terah's migration left Abram within the same religious environment.

23. "The person acquired" may refer to individuals and their families who joined Abram's entourage who in the absence of sons provided labor for the camp and later helped make up his fighting force of 318 "retainers, born into his household" (14:14). The Hebrew term for "retainers" appears only here and so is obscure. In modern Hebrew, the term has come to mean "apprentice" (Alkalay 1970).

24. J.P.S. "kinsman".

25. cf. Miller 1981:5-6 "Quite often we are faced here with gifted patients who have been praised and admired for their talents and their achievements...In everything they undertake they do well and often excellently; they are admired and envied; they are successful whenever they care to be - but all to no avail.

Behind all this lurks depression, the feeling of emptiness and self-alienation, and a sense that their life has no meaning. These dark feelings will come to the fore as soon as the drug of grandiosity fails...Then they are plagued by anxiety or deep feelings of guilt and shame. What are the reasons for such narcisstic disturbances in these gifted people?"

26. Probably near the town of Beitin, north of Jerusalem today in the occupied West Bank. (Weinfeld et. al. 1982).

27. Among the finds of the Dead Sea Scrolls was a midrashic elaboration of the night on the border of Egypt, including a warning dream to Abram and a poem by the Egyptians praising Sarai's beauty cf. Genesis Apocrphon (Mazar 1959).

28. Goldman (1988); Ochs (1977); and Teubel (1984) try to present events from Sarah's point of view. Teubel's "Sarah the Priestess: The First Matriarch of Genesis" argues that Sarah, a Mesopotamian Priestess as her name suggests, represented a disappearing non-partiarchal tradition and Gen. 18 carries traces of the rite "sacred marriage" (**hieros gamos**) between a priestess and the divinity, as "Goddess incarnate". She also suggests that the matriarchs **chose** to delay reproduction because of the patriarchal conditions they found in "exile" in Canaan.

29. 10:21 is grammatical ambiguous and may be read as Japheth being the oldest son, which would fit the listing of his descendants ahead of Ham and Shem (10:2f).

30. "Abram's disguise 'can' be countenanced in a good cause where power relationships are asymmetrical (cf. the excuses of the midwives about failing to kill Hebrew boys)" (Wildavsky 1984:245 41) since we know from ancient Egyptian texts that Abram's fears were at least on occasion justified. Note there is no mention of wives when Joseph's brothers go down to Egypt to purchase grain.

31. cf. my forthcoming "Disguise as a Prelude to Homecoming" in The Transcendant Function, ed. M. Matton, Daimon Verlag, Einsiedeln, Switzerland.

32. Some cultures have highly specific outcomes associated with brother-sister incest e.g. "According to traditional Navaho belief, sibling incest causes grand mal seizures." (Levy 1987:307).

33. cf. Rosenberg (1968:96): "Throughout the Abraham cycle, Abraham is shown severing from kin and household in more than one way; leaving his father's house, temporarily losing his kindred wife to a foreign king, expelling Hagar and Ishmael, offering up Isaac, burying Sarah. Erosion of the family seems a constant process and constant threat."

34. NB:The text states: "Abram went down to Egypt to sojourn there, for the famine was severe in the land" (12:10) and later adds: "From Egypt, Abram went up into the Negeb, with his wife and all he possessed, together with Lot" (13:1). Although the text seems to imply that Lot acocmpanied Abram into Egypt, it is not clearly stated. The Hebrew text "ve-Lot imo hanegba" "and Lot with him, into the south" (K.J) might just conceivably read that Abram joined up with Lot in the Negev "after" his exodus from Egypt.

35. The absence of a standardized list argues against an oral epic Biblical tradition, which as in the case of Serbian Epics and probably Homer, uses standardized epithets as a mnemonic device. (Lord 1968).

36. The main texts on hapiru/habiru are Bottero (1954); Greenberg (1955); De Vaux (1978:104-112). There is considerable controversy concerning the relation of "apiru" and Hebrew (Thompson 1974; Van Seters 1975); but see Muffs 1980 who argues strongly that Abram the Hebrew of Gen. 14 best fits the descriptons of "habiru": "if Abraham were a type of Habiru, and if Rowton's suggestion is correct that Habiru warriors preferred maquis forests, then Abraham's association with terebinth forests of Mamre would make excellent sense". (p. 106).

Likewise, Livingston (1987:297): "Their way of life as migrants and nomads is well documented by the Mari inscriptions and fits well with the biblical portrayal of the patriarchal lifestyle. Even the meaning of the word Hebrew is clarified by the Amorite verb "habuaru", to "emigrate", to "seek refuge".

37. Sarna (1966:122): "...Abraham's campaign in which a small group prevailed against powerful military opponents, is to be understood as signaling the fortunes of patriarch's descendants... There are many verbal echoes from 14 to 15: The Hebrew word for "shield" (magen v.1) is connected with Melchizedek's invocation of God who "delivered" (miggen 14:20) the patriarch's enemies..."rekhush"(14:21; 15:14) and "berit" (14:13; 15:18), Amorites (14:13; 15:16,21).

38. "At Nuzi, those who had no children adopted a stranger so as to ensure that they would be supported when they were old and to safeguard their funeral rites and the survival of their family and their inheritance. The adopted son was the "indirect heir", but if a natural son was born, the adopted son would forfeit his right to the main share in the inheritance. Thus, if Abraham had adopted a member of his household, the practice of Nuzi would explain Yahweh's reply (15:4) (De Vaux 1978:249).

39. cf Alexander (1983:19f): "Six important similarities can be observed between covenant of Noah and Abraham." He goes on to compare chapters 17 and 22, suggesting that the akeda was part of the covenant: Abraham is tested by God in order to ascertain whether or not he truly fulfils the conditions laid upon him in 17:1. Does Abraham walk before God? Is he blameless? Clearly the events of chapter 22 show beyond doubt the deep loyalty of Abraham to God. Obedience to God over rides paternal affection. As a result Abraham not only receives back his son but he also merits the divine ratification of the earlier promised covenant of circumcision.

40. Cf. Boyer (1987:17-32): "In the Hebraic-Christian tradition, unlike many others, the rainbow generally was looked upon with hope and confidence...A narrow interpretation of the passage can lead to the inference that no bow was seen before the time of the flood; but... exegetes interpreted the passage broadly as indicating that God here gave to the already familiar beauty of the rainbow a new significance, causing it to become a synbol of divine promise...The conception of the rainbow as a pathway or bridge has been widespread...Among the Japanese the rainbow is identified as the "Floating Bridge of Heaven"...Primitive Peruvians held the rainbow in such awe that they remained silent during its duration...Many primitive people viewed the rainbow with fear and misgiving, sharing with Homer the comparison of Iris to a serpent. In African mytholoy the rainbow is thought of as a giant snake that comes out after a rainfall to graze; and the hapless person upon whom he falls will be devoured...The shape of the bow, as well as its inescapability, caused primitive peoples of Nias to fear it as a huge net spread by a powerful spirit to catch their shadows or souls...it is wrong to point at the bow. One who points the finger at a rainbow may be struck by lightning, devlop an ulcer, or lose the finger...one who crosses, or passes directly under will change sex."

41. or "Abram put his faith in Yahweh, who counted this as making him justified".

42. cf. Jung (CW 8i, para. 82): "Symbolic process is an experience in images and of images" (quoted in Samuels 1985:119).

43. The Hebrew term, "bamakhazeh", translated as "in a vision" is the only prose use of this term - there are three references in Biblical poetry (Num 24:4,16; Ezek. 13:7). It is cognate to "khazon", the more common term in later prophets. It is also ambiguous whether the entire chapter contains one vision or several. Does Abram, in the dream vision, appear as "dreamer's ego" ask God, go outside, cut the pieces, fall asleep, behold the flaming torch or not?

The Hebrew word for "vision", "bamakhazeh" in modern Hebrew, would mean "in the drama" or "in the view", "view, scene, sight, vista, vision, spectacle, apparition, drama".

44. cf. Buber (1973:52-4): "I said to my partner: 'I have never been able to believe that this is a message of God. I do not believe it'...'What do you believe then?' 'I believe,' I replied without reflecting, 'that Samuel has misunderstood God.'

45. Contrast "to your descendants I will give the land" (12:7; 13:15) in incomplete action; "to your offspring I give this land" (15:18), completed action.

46. cf. Schafer (1980:35): "We are always telling stories about ourselves. In telling these self stories to others we may, for the most purposes, be said to be performing straightforward narrative actions. In saying that we also tell them to ourselves, however, we are enclosing one story within another. This is the story that there is a self to tell something to, a something or someone else serving as audience who is oneself or one's self."

47. Hasel (1981) gives an overview of the many meanings which have been attributed to the animal rite in Genesis 15, e.g. "... the passing between the animal pieces indicates the union of the covenant parties. This union has been conceived by some to be a "mystical-sacremental" one. Even where it is not so conceived, it is understood as a union that brings together into a close bond of fellowship two separated parties.

The "union" interpretation, whether "mystical-sacremental" or otherwise is felt to have significant weaknesses...A more prominent interpretation holds that the rite involving the cutting of animals with the subsequent passing between the "disjecta membra" transfers life to the contracting parties...the pieces of the animals absorbed divine power when the deity passed between them. This power or life force is subsequently absorbed by the consuming of the meat of the "disjecta membra" in a sacred meal. In this way life is transferred to the human party of the covenant...

Strictly speaking the animal rite in Gen 15:9-10, 17 is still without an exact extra-biblical parallel...We suggest that the animal cutting...is designated a "covenant ratification sacrifice". It differs from normal sacrifices and also from the sacrificial rites with their covenant rituals in Exod. 24:3-8. The killing and sectioning of the animals by Abram is the sacrificial "preparation" for the subsequent divine "ratification" of the covenant by Yahweh, who in passing between the pieces irrevocably pledges the fulfillment of his covenant promised to the patriarch. The initiative of Yahweh remains in the foreground both in the instruction for the "covenant ratification sacrifice" (Gen. 15:9-10) and in the act of "berit" ratification itself (v 17)...Certain basic features of this covenant ratification rite are most closely paralleled only in aspects of the function of animal rites of extant early second millenium treaty texts.

48. "I am treating the swooping down of birds as "an evil omen (Vergil, Aeneid, III, 235ff) threatening to thwart the conclusion of the covenant" (Van Rad 1976). But cf. Sarna for a different view: "Nor is there any indication of the role of the birds. Are they a relic of some technique of obtaining oracles? or since the promise of posterity plays so prominent a part, are they perhaps fertility symbols, familiar to us from Akkadian, Canaanite and Greek mythological texts?" (Sarna op. cit). Unburied corpse is a universal 'image of ultimate horror'.

The uncut birds of the covenant, then, contrast with the birds of prey. Symbols of hope and wholeness to contrast with image of hoplelessness and destruction/death.

49. cf. "Although the hero does not attain his initial aspiration, he is ultimately victorious: he confronts his profound inner faults, accepts them as part of himself and of humanity and is to some degree transformed into a nobler person. The personal transformation outweighs the worldly defeat and suffering...A man's new creativity in middle adulthood comes in part from his new relationship to his own destructiveness and from an intensification of the loving, life-affirming aspects of the self." (Levinson 1977:225f).

50. For an excellent futuristic version of a culture with Hagar-like "surrogate motherhood" written from her point of view, cf. Margaret Attwood, The

Handmaid's Tale: "...Why does she envy me. She doesn't speak to me, unless she can't avoid it. I am a reproach to her, and a necessity...How she must hate me..." (p. 13,86).

51. The clash between a mother's and a father's right to name the newborn is witnessed in the birth of Benjamin, The dying Rachel names the child Ben-oni ("son of my suffering" (or, "strength") but "his father named him Benjamin" ("Son of the right hand" or "son of the south"). (J.P.S. translation and footnote 35:18)

52. Five other Ishmaels are listed (cf. II Kings 25:25; Jer. 40-41; Ezra 10:22; I Chronicles 8:38;9:44; II Chronicles 19:11; 23:1;1) and in Talmud (cf. R. Ishmael) Traditional Jewish naming practices were an important source of intergenerational continuity (Zborowski & Herzog 1952), which has been broken in contemporary secular Israel by neologistic naming (Abramovitch & Bilu 1985).

53. In 20:2 Avimelech is called "King of Gerar"; the Avimelech of 26:8 is called "King of the Philistines".

54. Hebrew legend, Midrash, includes tales of reconciliation between Abraham and Ishmael, as in the story that Abraham visits Ishmael's camp, having promised Sarah that he will not descend from his donkey. Arriving at the camp, he meets Ishmael's wife, who receives him badly and leaves a message for his son that this tent peg (i.e. his wife) is faulty. Ishmael understands his father and changes wives, and when a second visit is paid, the father leaves the message that now he has "a sturdy" tent peg.

55. "While this maternal shelter has to be relinquished by the young male, he will still be in need of some protection in the struggles of life that loom ahead, he will require a 'shield', as it were, which he carries with him. The shield-shelter simile sums up many of the problems facing the adolescent at puberty, and circumcision and initiation are as much concerned with providing the one as with separation from the other" (Seligman 1965:6). Likewise, "The renunciation of the foreskin-boundary was experienced as a 'sacrifice' of the secure protection of the mother and of the pleasure of omnipotent infantile sexual fantasies. It meant giving up narcisstic and incestuous pleasure in order to achieve love for a woman as object, the foreskin becoming a ring to put on a wife's finger. The sexuality to be sacrificed was felt as being unclean..." (Hobson 1961:10)

56. "Yitschak" is used in place of the conventional "Isaac" to preserve the etymological significance of his name.

57. "And Abraham said to God, "Oh, that Ishmael might live by Your favor!" (17:17-18) is literally, "Would Ishmael live before you", which I interpret as a latent death anxiety or paternal "death wish" projected onto the Lord, an unconscious expression of his ambivalence that having waited so long so little was achieved; having mentored this unworthy disciple, he secretly desired to get rid of an ungrateful protegé.

Death wishes and succession also lie at the heart of the break between Freud and Jung, specifically whether Jung had "death wishes" toward Freud:

> *"Why are you so interested in these corpses?" he (Freud) asked me (Jung) several times. He was inordinately vexed by the whole thing and during one such conversation, while we were having dinner together, he suddenly fainted. Afterwards he said to me that he was convinced that all this chatter about corpses meant that I had death-wishes toward him...*

In a similar connection Freud once more suffered a fainting fit in my presence. This was during the Psychoanalytic Congress in Munich in 1912. Someone had turned the conversation to Amenophis IV (Ikhnaton). The point was made that as a result of his negative attitude towards his father he had destroyed his father's cartouches on the steles, and that at the back of his great creation of a monoththeistic religion lurked a father complex. This sort of thing irritated me, and I attempted to argue that Amenophis had been a creative and profoundly religious person whose acts could not be explained by personal resistences toward his father. On the contrary, I said, he had held the memory of his father in honor, and his zeal for destruction had been directed only against the name of the god Amon, which he had annihilated everywhere; it was also chiseled out of the cartouches of his father Amon-hotep. Moreover, other pharaohs had replaced the names of their actual or divine forefathers on monuments and status by their own, feeling that they had a right to do so since they were incarnations of the same god. Yet they, I pointed out, had inaugurated neither a new style nor a new religion.

At that moment Freud slid off his chair in a faint...the fantasy of father-murder was common to both cases. (Jung 1963:180-1).

58. Deut. 23:1-9 describes those who are prohibited from being admitted to the "assembly of Yahweh" i.e public worship. The prohibitions describe an exclusionary hierarchy. Those unclean by reason of nocturnal emission, especially at times of war, must stay out of camp, until after washing, and may only return at sunset. Men with genital damage (crushed testicles or severed penis) are excluded, but Bastards (mamzeir), Moabites and Ammonites are banned forever, "not even their descendants to the tenth generation may be admitted"; while Edomites (descendants of Esau) and Egyptians (former because he is your brother; the latter because you were a stranger in his land (just as Hebrews were strangers at first in the Promised Land - and retain an ethical concern with the stranger) "the third generation of children born to these may be admitted" (Deut.23:8-9).

59. cf. Rachel's personal cry "Give me children or I shall die" (Gen. 30:1) is a poignant evocation of the need for biological continuity and maternal fulfilment.

60. cf. Blenkinsopp (1980:129), who considers 18:23-32 as "a midrash on the destruction of Sodom occasioned by the destruction of Jerusalem in 586 B.C.E. and the theological problems to which this event gave rise.... Abraham recapitulates and vindicates the role of the prophet who attempts, unsuccessfully, to intercede on behalf of the doomed city from which only a small remnant, the family of Lot, will escape."

61. cf. Lifton (1979).

62. cf. Sarna (1966:161): "The demand of God is presented as something extraordinary, something that a man would not dream of doing on his own initiative, and something that tries the believer to the utmost so that his response is by no means predictable."

63. In Hebrew text, the normal syntatctic order (verb-subject-object) is inverted (subject-verb-object) and a definite article "ha" is added to "elohim" God. Both devices serve to stress that it was **God** who initiated the test.
cf. Speiser 1964:162; Sarna 1966:165, n. 40.

64. "Violence is always present in human groups, threatening to fragment the self, threatening to split the group, threatening to invade another group. The hero voluntarily undergoes an ordeal to overcome his own violence, calms the violence of others, counters the power of death to destroy meaning, strives for justice, and values both the single person and the sacred power of the group.

The hero never submits passively to sacred order. Indeed, it is the friction of his asserting the values of both the personal and the social, the old and the new, us and them, that makes time blaze with meaning, illuminating the drama of their collision in the human soul. The hero tries to protect both change and social order against violence. He opposes the schism of "us and them". (Shapiro 1984:206).

For a different but complementary view of relation of "Violence and the Sacred" as a form of collective displacement, cf. Girard (1972), "Society is seeking to deflect upon a relatively indifferent victim, a "sacrificeable" victim, the violence that would otherwise be vented on its own members, the people it most desires to protect...the sacrifice serves to protect the entire community from its own violence, to chose victims outside of itself...Ritual, in general, and sacrificial rites in particular, assume essential roles in societies that lack a firm judicial order" (Girard 1972:4f). Girard opens his book with the paradoxical assertion that sacred victims are sacred only because they are to be killed and thus if sacrifice resembles criminal activity violence, it also contains an element of mystery.

Cf. Wildavsky (1984:118-122) for discussion of the parallel between Akeda and Passover Exodus, he goes on following van Rad's (1976:244) claim that "when Israel read and related this story in later times it could only see itself represented by Isaac i.e. laid on Yahweh's altar": "Abraham has his knife at the throat of the entire Jewish people...The Akeda is an earlier version of the Golden Calf. As far as may be understood it is a justification for the sacrifice of an entire generation in order to create a people able to fulfill its promise. The entire people - that is, Isaac - is to be offered to the God who stands for the unity of the people. The risk, the Akeda instructs us, is worth taking...Ram to ram, sacrifice to sacrifice, renewal to renewal, blood to blood, from the denial of man's right to take life, as if he were a god, to the worship of the pseudo-good, the idolator, pharaoh, the exodus is encapsulated in the Akeda" (Wildavksy 1984:121).

cf. also the excellent and widely acclaimed Spiegel (1979): The Last Trial: On the Legends and Lore of he Command to Abraham to Offer Isaac as a Sacrifice: The Akeda. Translated from the Hebrew, with an Introduction, by Judah Goldin.

65. Hebrew Bible commentators make many suggestions concerning Isaac's age, the most extreme being 37 to link up with the death of Sarah in the following chapter, Sarah dying at hearing news of the akeda. Other suggest age five which seems too young considering the wood and the type of question. Ibn

Ezra and Reik (1961) both together suggest a possible realistic age of 13, the year of Bar Mitzvah, in later times age of male ritual initiation.

66. Contrast the differing translations of difficult verse 22:14: "And Abraham named that site Adonia-yireh (i.e. 'the Lord will see') cf. v.8), whence the present saying, 'On the mount of the Lord there is vision' (J.P.S.). "And Abraham called the name of that place Jehovah-jireh: as it is said to this day, In the mount of the Lord it shall be seen" (King James): "Abraham called this place, 'Yahweh provides' and hence the saying today: On the mountain Yahweh provides." (Jerusalem Bible).

67. A recent study of men who murder their children revealed that most suffered from severe mental impairment, psychosis, neurological deficits, substance abuse and/or mental retardation. On the other hand, like Abraham, most were not physically abusive until the killing, exhibiting what the authors term "isolated explosive behavior". It must be noted that as part of child abuse syndrome, mothers are responsible for many more deaths than fathers (Campion, Cravens & Covan 1988).

68. cf. Gonzales (1967:117): "High on Moriah, Isaac had just been born...The Isaac born on Moriah was doubly the son of Abraham's faith. The father obtained him, not as the fruit of his aged flesh, but rather as the creation of his youthful faith."

69. This passage is taken as the Scriptural basis for a peculiar kabbalistic mortuary rite in which just prior to burial the corpse is circumambulated by a quorum of 10 men after which each time, coins, or other valuables are thrown to the various directions, these being the "gifts" given to the "son of the concubines" in kabbalistic metaphor, unincarnated demons engendered by man's seminal ejaculations. For more on this strange rite, (cf. Scholem 1965:154-7; Abramovitch 1986; 1991).

70. "Psalm of the Jealous God", Henry Abramovitch, in Voice Within the Ark: The Modern Jewish Poets, ed. H. Schwartz and A. Rudolf. Avon:NY 1981.

BIBLIOGRAPHY

Abramovitch, Henry (1975) "Report on the Living and Dead" in J. Berry and W. Lonner (eds.) Applied Cross Cultural Psychology. Amsterdam: Swets.

Abramovitch, Henry (1986) "There are No Words: Two Greek-Jewish Survivors of Auschwitz" Psychoanalytical Psychology 3(3):201-216.

Abramovitch, Henry (1986) "The Clash of Values in the Jerusalem Funeral: A Participant-Observer Study of a "Hevra Kadisha" Proceedings of the Ninth World Congress of Jewish Studies. Jerusalem: World Union of Jewish Studies.

Abramovitch, Henry (1987) "Death" in A.A. Cohen and P. Mendes-Flohr (eds.). Contemporary Jewish Religious Thought: Original Essays on Critical Concepts, Movements and Belief. NY: Charles Scribners' Sons.

Abramovitch, Henry (1991) "Jerusalem Funeral As A Microcosm of Mismeeting Between Religious and Secular". In Zvi Sobel and Benjamin Beit-Hallahmi (eds.) Tradition Innovation Conflict: Judaism and Jewishness in Contemporary Israel. Albany: SUNY Press.

Abramovitch, H. and Bilu Y. (1985) "Visitational Dreams and Naming Practices among Moroccan Jews in Israel". Jewish Journal of Sociology. 23(1): 13-22.

Adar, Zvi (1959) The Biblical Narrative. Jerusalem: Jewish Agency.

Albright, W.F. (1963) "Abram the Hebrew: A New Archeological Interpretation" Bulletin of the American Society for Oriental Research (BASOR). 163: 36-54.

Alcalay, R. (1970) The Complete Hebrew-English Dictionary. Jerusalem: Massada.

Alexander, T.D. (1982) "A Literary Analysis of the Abraham Narrative". Ph.D. Thesis Belfast-University.

Alexander, T.D. "Genesis 22 and the Covenant of Circumcision" JSOT 25: 17-22.

Allport, Gordon (1942) The Use of Personal Documentation in Psychological Science. NY: SSRC.

Alter, Robert (1981) The Art of Biblical Narrative NY: Basic Books.

Alter, Robert and Kermode, Frank (Eds.) (1987) Literary Guide to the Bible. Cambridge: Harvard University Press.

Andriolo, Karin R. (1973) "A Structural Analysis of Geneology and World View in the Old Testament" American Anthropologist 75(5): 1657-1669.

Andriolo, Karin R. (1981) "Myth and History: A General Model and its Application to the Bible". American Anthropologist. 83(2): 261-284.

Attwood, Margret (1985) The Handmaid's Tale. Toronto: McClelland and Stewart.

Bakan, David (1971) Disease, Pain and Suffering. Boston: Beacon Press.

Bakan, David (1979) And They Took Themselves Wives: The Emergence of Patriarchy in Western Civilization. NY: Harper & Row.

Bar-Efrat, Shimon (1979) The Art of the Biblical Story (Hebrew). Tel Aviv: Tel Aviv University Press.

Barth, F. (1954) "Father's brothers' daughter marriage in Kurdistan". South West Journal of Anthropology. 10:11-17.

Beck, S. (1963) "Abraham's Ordeal: Creation of a New Reality" Psychoanalytic Review. 50: 335-344.

Benjamin, Walter (1969) "The Task of the Translator" in Illuminations ed. Hanna Arendt (trans. Harry Zohn). NY: Schocken, pp. 69-82.

Berelson, B. and Steiner, G.A. (1964) Human Behavior: An Inventory of Scientific Findings. NY: Harcourt, Brace and World.

Besançon, A. (1974) "Freud, Abraham and Laius" in Les Chemins de l'Anti-Oedipe. ed. J. Chasseguet - Smirel, pp. 23-38. Toulouse: Privat.

Blenkinsopp, Joseph (1980) "Abraham and the Righteous of Sodom" Journal of Jewish Studies. 119-132.

Bloch, Maurice (1971) Placing the Dead. NY: Seminar Press.

Bloch, Maurice (1986) From Blessing to Violence: History and Ideology in the Circumcision Ritual of the Merina of Madagascar. Cambridge Studies in Social Anthropology. Cambridge: Cambridge University Press.

Bloch, Maurice and Parry, Jonathan (Eds.) (1982) Death and the Regeneration of Life. Cambridge, U.K.: Cambridge University Press.

Bloom, Harold (Ed.) (1986) Genesis: Modern Critical Interpretations. NY: Chelsea House.

Boszormenyi-Nagry, Ivan and Krasner, Barbara (1986) Between Give and Take: A Clinical Guide to Contextual Therapy. NY: Brunner Mazel Publishers.

Boyer, Carl B. (1987) The Rainbow: From Myth to Mathematics. Princeton: Princeton University Press.

Brams, Steven J. (1980) Biblical Games: A Structural Analysis of Stories in the Old Testament. Cambridge, Mass.: M.I.T. Press.

Brenner, Athalya (1983) The Israelite Woman: Social Role and Literary Type in Biblical Narrative. Sheffield: JSOT.

Buber, Martin (1946) Moses: The Revelation and the Covenant. NY: Schocken reprinted with a new Introduction (1988). Atlantic Highlands, N.J.: Humanities Press.

Buber, Martin (1963) "Abraham the Seer" in On the Bible ed. Nahum Glatzer: NY: Schocken (cf. "Abraham the Seer" trans. Sophie Meyer Judaism 5(4). Fall 1956).

Buber, Martin (1965) The Knowledge of Man: A Philosophy of the Interhuman. NY: Harper and Row.

Buber, Martin (1973) Meetings, edited with an Introduction and Bibliography by Maurice Friedman. LaSalle, Illinois: Open Court Publishing.

Buhler, Charlotte (1935) "The Curve of Life as Studied in Biography". Journal of Applied Psychology. 19: 405-9.

Buhler, Charlotte (1968) The Course of Human Life: A Study of Goals in Humanistic Perspective. NY: Springer.

Butler, Robert N. (1968) "The Life Review: An Interpretation of Reminiscence in the Aged" in Bernice L. Neugarten (ed.) Middle Age and Aging. Chicago: University of Chicago Press. pp. 486-96.

Buttler, Sandra (1979) Conspiracy of Silence: The Trauma of Incest. NY: Bantam.

Campion, J., Cravens, J.M. and Covan, F. (1988) "A Study of Filicidal Men" American Journal of Psychiatry. 145(4): 1141-4.

Cassuto, V. (1964) From Noah to Abraham. Jerusalem: The Magnes Press.

Coats, G.W. (1983) Genesis, with an Introduction to Narrative Literature. Grand Rapids: Eerdmans.

Cohen, H. Hirsch (1974) The Drunkedness of Noah. University of Alabama Press.

Collins, A.Y. (ed.) (1985) Feminist Perspectives on Biblical Scholarship. Chico, Ca: Scholars Press.

Crapanzano, Vincent (1977) "The Life History in Anthropological Field Work", Anthropology and Humanism Quarterly. 2: 3-7.

Crapanzano, Vincent (1980) Tuhami: Portrait of a Moroccan. Chicago: University of Chicago Press.

Dahlberg, Bruce T. (1982) "The Unity of Genesis" in K. Gros Louis (Ed.) Literary Interpretations of Biblical Narratives v. 2 Nashville: Abingdon, pp. 126-34.

Danforth, Loring M. (1982) The Death Rituals of Rural Greece. Princeton: Princeton University Press.

de Waard, Jon and Nida, Eugene A. (1986) From One Language to Another: Functional Equivalence in Bible Translation. Nashville: Thomas Nelson Publishers.

Dollard, John (1935) Criteria for the Life History. New Haven: Yale University Press.

Donaldson, Mara E. (1981) "Kinship Theory in the Patriarchal Narratives. The Case of the Barren Wife". Journal of the American Academy of Religion. 49: 77-87.

Douglas, Mary (1969) Purity and Danger: An Analysis of Concepts of Pollution and Taboo. 2nd Ed. London: Routledge and Kegan Paul.

Dreifuss, G. (1965) "A Psychological Study of Circumcision in Judaism". Journal of Analytic Psychology. 10(1): 23-32.

Dundes, Alan (Ed.) (1984) Sacred Narrative. Chicago: University of Chicago Press.

Dworkin, Andrea (1987) Intercourse. London: Arrow Books.

Edwards, Jay D. (1978) The Afro-American Trickster Tale: A Structural Analysis. Bloomington: Indiana University Press.

Erikson, Erik H. (1963) Childhood and Society Revised Ed. NY: Norton.

Erikson, Erik H. (1968) "On the Nature of Psycho-Historical Evidence: In Search of Gandhi". Daedalus. 97(3): 695-730.

Erikson, Erik H. (1968) Identity: Youth and Crisis. NY: Norton.

Erikson, Erik H. (1975) Life History and the Historical Moment. NY: Norton.

Fackenheim, Emil (1976) "Abraham and the Kantians" in Encounters Between Modern Philosophy and Judaism. Chapter 2, pp. 31-77. NY: Basic.

Fein, Leonard (1989). "Nonorthodoxy Does Not Mean Uncommanded". Sh'ma, April 14, 1984, 19/372.

Fewell, D.N. (1987) "Feminist Readings of the Hebrew Bible" JSOT 39: 75-87.

Fishbane, Michael (1979) Text and Texture: Close Readings of Selected Biblical Texts. NY: Schocken.

Fokkelman, J.P. (1975) Narrative Art in Genesis: Specimens of Stylistic and Structural Analysis. Amsterdam: Van Gorcum, Assem.

Fokkelman, J.P. "Genesis" in Alter and Kermode (1981).

Forsyth, Dan W. (1991) "Sibling Rivalry, Aesthetic Sensibility, and Social Structure in Genesis". ETHOS 1991.

Fox, Everett (1983) In the Beginning: A New English Rendition of the Book of Genesis. Translated with Commentary and Notes. NY: Schocken.

Frenkel, Else (1936) "Studies in Biographic Psychology". Character and Personality. 5: 1-34.

Friedman, Maurice (1983) Martin Buber's Life and Work: The Middle Years. NY: Dutton.

Friedman, Richard Elliot (1988) Who Wrote the Bible? London: Cape.

Fritz, Charles E. (1961) "Disasters" in R.K. Merton and R.A. Nisbet (eds.) Contemporary Social Problems. NY: Harcourt Brace.

Gabel, J.B. and Wheeler, C.B. (1986) The Bible as Literature: An Introduction. Oxford: Oxford University Press.

Geertz, C. (1973) The Interpretation of Cultures. NY: Basic Books.

Gevirtz, S. (1969) "Abram's 318". Israel Exploration Journal. 19: 110-113.

Girard, René (1972) Violence and the Sacred (trans. Patrick Gregory), Baltimore: Johns Hopkins University Press.

Glassman, Eugene H. (1981) The Translation Debate: What Makes a Bible Translation Good? Downers Grove, IL.

Goldman-Amirav, Anna (1988) "Behold the Lord Hath Restrained Me from Bearing".
Reproductive and Genetic Engineering. 1(3): 275-9.

Gonzalez, Angel, Abraham: Father of Believers. London.

Gordon, C.H. (1965) The Common Background of Greek and Hebrew Civilization.
NY: Atheneum.

Gottcent, J.H. (1986) The Bible: A Literary Study. London: Twayne.

Gottwald, N.K. (1980) Tribes of Yahweh: Sociology of the Religion of Liberated
Israel 1250-1050 B.C.E. Maryknoll, NY: Orbis.

Gottwald, N.K. (1986) The Hebrew Bible: A Socio-Literary Introduction.
Philadelphia: Fortress Press.

Graves, R. and Patai R. (1964) Hebrew Myths. NY: McGraw-Hill.

Greenstein, Edward L. (1983) "Theories of Modern Bible Translation". Prooftexts.
3: 9-39.

Greenwood, David C. (1985) Structuralism and the Biblical Text. Berlin: Mouton.

Grene, D. and Lattimore, R. (Eds.) (1954) The Complete Greek Tragedies.
Chicago: University of Chicago Press.

Gros Louis, Kenneth R.R. (1982) "Abraham I and II" in Gros Louis, K. and
Ackerman, J.S. (Eds.) Literary Intepretations of Biblical Narrative 2 vol.
Nashville: Abingdon.

Hallo, W.W. and Simpson W.K. (1971) The Ancient Near East: A History NY:
Harcourt, Brace and Janovich.

Hasel, Gerhard F. (1981) "The Meaning of the Animal Rite in Genesis 15". JSOT.
19: 61-78.

Heller, Joseph (1984) God Knows. London: Cape.

Herman, Judith Lewis and Hirschman, Lisa (1982) Father-Daughter Incest.
Cambridge, Mass: Harvard University Press.

Hobson, R.F. (1961) "Psychology Aspects of Circumcision". Journal of Analytical Psychology. 6: 5-33.

Hunter, Alastair G. (1986) "Father Abraham: A Structural and Theological Study of the Yahwist's Presentation of the Abraham Material". JSOT. 35: 3-27.

Jung, C.G. (1963) Memories Dreams Reflections. ed. Aniela Jaffe - NY: Pantheon.

Kalish, Richard A. (1985) Death, Grief and Caring Relationships. 2nd ed. Monterey, Ca: Brooks and Cole.

Kramer, S.N. (1940) Lamentation over the City of Ur. Chicago: University of Chicago Press.

Lang, Bernhard (Ed.) (1985) Anthropological Approaches to the Old Testament. Philadelphia: Fortress Press.

Langress, L.L. and Frank G. (1981). Lives: An Anthropological Approach to Biography. Novato, Ca: Chandler and Sharp.

Lauterberg, J.Z. (1970) "The Naming of Children in Jewish Folklore Ritual and Practice" in Studies in Jewish Law, Custom and Folklore. NY: Ktav.

Leach, E. (1969) Genesis as Myth and Other Essays. London: Cape.

Leach, E. and Aycock, D.A. (1983) Structuralist Interpretations of Biblical Myth. Cambridge: Cambridge University Press.

Levav, I., Krasnoff, L., Dohrennerd, B. (1981) "Israeli Peri Life Events Scale: Ratings of Events by a Community Sample". Israeli Journal of Medical Sciences. 17: 176-183.

Levinson, Daniel J. (1978) The Seasons of a Man's Life. NY: Knopf.

Levy, Jerrold E. (1987) "Psychological and Social Problems of Epileptic Children in Four Southwestern Indian Tribes". Journal of Community Psychology. 15: 307-15.

Lifton, Robert J. (1971) History and Human Survival. NY: Random House.

Lifton, Robert J. (1979) The Broken Connection: On Death and the Continuity of Life. NY: Simon and Schuster.

Lister, R. (1982) "Forced Silence". American Journal of Psychiatry. 139:871-875.

Livingston, G.H. (1987) The Pentateuch in its Cultural Environment 2nd Ed. Grand Rapids, MI: Baker Book House.

Lord, A.B. (1968) The Singer of Tales. NY: Atheneum.

McConnell, F. (1986) The Bible and Narrative Tradition. Oxford: Oxford University Press.

Miller, Alice (1981) The Drama of The Gifted Child. NY: Basic Books.

Muffs, Yochanan (1980) "Abraham the Noble Warrior: Patriarchal Politics and Laws of War in Ancient Israel". Journal of Jewish Studies. 81-107.

Muhawi, Ibrahim and Kanaanan, Sharif (1989) Speak Bird, Speak Again: Palestinian Arab Folktales. Berkeley and Los Angeles: University of California Press.

Neumann, Erich (1954) The Origins and History of Consciousness. Bollingan Series XLII. Princeton: Princeton University Press.

Nidtich, Susan (1987) Underdogs and Tricksters: A Prelude to Biblical Folklore. NY: Harper and Row.

Oden, Robert (1983) "Jacob as Father, Husband and Nephew: Kinship Stuides and the Patriarchal Narratives". Journal of Biblical Literature. 102: 189-205.

Orlinsky, Harry (1966) "The Rage to Translate" in Genesis: NJV Translation. NY: Harper and Row pp. ix-xxviii.

Ortner, Susan (1974) "Is female to male as nature is to culture?" in M. Rosaldo and L. Lumphese (Eds.) Woman, Culture and Society. Stanford: Stanford University Press, pp. 67-88.

Parrot, A. (1962) Abraham et Son Temps. Neuchatel: Editions Delacroix.

Penfield, W. (1935) "Abraham of the Chaldees" Bulletin of the History of Medicine.

Pitt-Rivers, Julian (1978) The Fate of Shechem or The Politics of Sex: Essays in the Anthropology of the Mediterranean. Cambridge: Cambridge University Press.

Preminger, A. and Greenstein, E. (Eds.) (1986) The Hebrew Bible in Literary Criticism. NY: Ungar.

Pritchard, J.B. (1969) Ancient Near Eastern Texts Relating to the Old Testament 3rd Ed. with supplement. Princeton: Princeton University Press.

Radday, Yehuda (1981) "Chiasmus in Hebrew Biblical Narrative" in J.W. Welch (Ed.) Chiasmus in Antiquity. Hildershum.

Radday, Yehuda and Shore, Haim (1985) Genesis: An Authorship Study in Computer Assisted Statistical Linguistics. Rome: Biblical Institute Press.

Radin, P. (1956) The Trickster NY: Schocken.

Reik, T. (1961) The Temptation NY: Braziller.

Rensburg, Gary A. (1986) The Redaction of Genesis. Winona Lake, In: Eisenbrauns.

Rogerson, J.W. (1978) Anthropology and the Old Testament. Oxford: Basil Blackwells.

Rosenberg, Joel (1986) "Is There a Story of Abraham?" in King and Kin: Political Allegory in the Hebrew Bible. Bloomington: Indiana University Press. Ch. II, pp. 69-98.

Ross, John M. (1982) "Oedipus and the Laius Complex". Psychoanalytic Study of the Child. v.37. New Haven: Yale University Press.

Rouiller, Gregoire (1978) "The Sacrifice of Isaac Genesis 22: 1-19, First Reading" in Bovan and Rouiller (eds.) Exegesis: Problems of Method and Exercises in Reading Genesis 22 and Luke 15 (trans. Donald G. Miller) Pittsburgh: Pickwick.

Rudin-O'brasky, Talia (1982) The Patriarchs in Hebron and Sodom (Hebrew). Jerusalem: Simor.

Russell, Letty M. (ed.) (1985) Feminist Interpretation of the Bible. Philadelphia: Westminister.

Said, Edward W. (1981) Beginnings: Intention and Method. NY: Basic Books.

Samuels, Andrew (1985) Jung and the Post-Jungians. London: Routledge and Kegan Paul.

Sarna, Nahum M. (1966) Understanding Genesis. NY: McGraw and Hill.

Sarna, Nahum M. (1982) "The Anticipatory Use of Information as a Literary Feature of the Genesis Narrative" in R. Freedman (ed.) The Creation of Sacred Literature. Berkeley and Los Angeles: University of California.

Schafer, R. (1980) Critical Inquiry. 6:35-40.

Scholem, G. (1965) "Tradition and New Creation in the Ritual of the Kabbalists" in On the Kaballah and its Symbolism. NY: Schocken.

Seligman, Paul (1965) "Some Notes on the Collective Significance of Circumcision and Allied Practices". Journal of Analytic Psychology. 10(1): 5-21.

Shapiro, Steven A. (1984) Manhood: A New Definition. NY: Putnam's Sons.

Shinan, Avigdor and Zakovitch, Yair (1983) Gen. 10:10-20 in the Bible, the Old Versions and the Ancient Jewish Literature (Hebrew). Research Projects of the Institute of Jewish Studies. Jerusalem: Hebrew University.

Shoham, S. Giora (1976) "The Isaac Syndrome". American Imago. 33(4): 329-49.

Silver, D.J. (1982) Images of Moses. NY: Basic Books.

Speiser, E.A. (1964) Genesis: The Anchor Bible. Chicago: Random House.

Spiegel, Shalom (1967) The Last Trial: On the Legends and Lore of the Command to Abraham to Offer Isaac as a Sacrifice: The Akeda trans. with an introduction by Judah Goldin. NY: Behrman.

Spiro, M. (1983) "Thirty Years of Kibbutz Research" in S. Krausz (ed.) The Sociology of the Kibbutz. New Brunswick, NJ: Transaction.

Spitz, Ellen Handler (1988) "The Inescapability of Tragedy". Bulletin of the Meninger Foundation. 52(2): 377-382.

Steinzaltz, Adin (1980) "Our Father Abraham" in Biblical Personalities (Hebrew). Tel Aviv: Universita Meshuderet, pp. 9-15.

Sternberg, Meir (1985) The Poetics of Biblical Narrative. Bloomington: Indiana University Press.

Storr, Anthony (1988). Churchill's Black Dog, Kafka's Mice and Other Phenomena of The Human Mind, NY: Grove Press.

Talmon, Yonina (1972) Family and Community in the Kibbutz. Cambridge, Mass: Harvard University Press.

Teubel, Savira (1984) Sarah the Priestess: The First Matriarch of Genesis. Athens, Ohio: Swallow Press.

Trible, Phyllis (1985) Texts of Terror: Literary Feminist Readings of Biblical Narrative. Philadelphia: Fortress Press.

Thompson, T.L. (1974) The Historicity of the Patriarchal Narrative. The Quest for the Historical Abraham. Berlin: BZAW #133.

Thompson, T.L. (1987) The Origin Tradition of Ancient Israel: The Literary Formation of Genesis and Exodus 1-23. Sheffield: JSOT Press.

Van Rad, Gerhard (1972) Genesis: A Commentary. Revised Ed. London: SCM Press.

Van Seters, John (1975) Abraham in History and Tradition. New Haven, Ct.: Yale University Press.

Vaux, Roland de (1978) The Early History of Israel (trans. David Smith). Philadelphia: Westminster.

Vawter, Bruce (1977) On Genesis: A New Reading. Garden City, NY: Doubleday.

Weinfeld, M. Avishur, Y. and Klein, Y. (1982) The Book of Genesis (Hebrew). Jerusalem: Revivim.

Wellisch, E. (1954) Isaac and Oedipus. London: Routledge and Kegan Paul.

Wenham, G.J. (1988) "Genesis: An Authorship Study and Current Pentateuchal Criticism". JSOT. 42: 3-18.

Westerman, Claus (1980) The Promises to the Fathers: Studies in the Patriarchal Narratives. (trans. David E. Green). Philadelphia: Fortress Press.

Westerman, Claus (1985) Genesis 12-36 (trans. John J. Sullivan). Minneapolis, MN: Augusberg.

White, Robert W. (1952) Lives in Progress: A Study of the Natural Growth of Personality. NY: Holt.

White, Robert W. (Ed.) (1960) The Study of Lives: Essays in Personality in Honor of Henry A. Murray. NY: Atheneum.

Wildavsky, Aaron (1984) The Nursing Father: Moses as a Political Leader. University of Alabama Press.

Wilson, R.R. (1975) "The Old Testament Geneologies in Recent Research". Journal of Biblical Literature. 94: 169-89.

Wilson, R.R. (1977) Geneology and History in The Biblical World. New Haven: Yale University Press.

Wilson, R.R. (1984) Sociological Approaches to the Old Testament. Philadelphia: Fortress Press.

Wolfenstein, Victor (1967) The Revolutionary Personality. Princeton: Princeton University Press.

Wooley, Leonard (1936) Abraham. London: Penguin.

Zborowski, M. and Herzog, E. (1952) Life is with People: The Culture of the Shetetl. NY: Schocken.

Zeligs, Dorothy (1974) Psychoanalysis and the Bible: A Study in Depth of Seven Leaders. NY: Bloch.

Index

Index of Biblical References

Genesis

Genesis

Deutoronomy

28:58-63	138n.
29:21-25	109
34:6	126

Joshua

5:2-5	95
7:1-26	102
11:3	69
17:15	69
19:47	73
24:29	115

Judges

2:22	118
3:1, 4	118
6:39	118
18:28-31	73

Samuel

I 3:4	119
I 4:11	35
I 8:1-22	35
I 14:24-45	36
I 20:30-1	36
I 21:13-16	63
I 28:8	63
I 30	75
I 31:6	36
II 1:7	119
II 13:14	63
II 19	36
II 19:2	126
II 21	81

Kings

I 1:5-6	36
I 1:7-39	36
I 2:1-9	126
I 9:20-23	69
I 12:10	36
I 16:16-26	90
I 17:17	115
I 21:1	115
II 17:7-23	102
II 25:25	85

Jeremiah

23:14	109
40:41	85
43:8-22	81
49:18	109
50:40	109

Isaiah

1:9-10	109
13:19-20	109
58:9	119

Ezekiel

16:46f.	109
37:	128